THINKING, FEELING, BEHAVING

An Emotional Education
Curriculum for Children

GRADES 1-6

ANN VERNON

RESEARCH PRESS
2612 North Mattis Avenue
Champaign, Illinois 61821

Cover design by Jack Davis
Composition by Shepard Poorman Communications Corporation

ISBN 0–87822–305–3

Library of Congress Catalog Card Number 89–60713

CONTENTS

Foreword   vii

Acknowledgments   ix

Introduction   1

Grades 1–2

SELF-ACCEPTANCE

1 People Hunt   11
2 People Poster   13
3 Can Do, Can't Do   15
4 Changes, Changes   17
5 Oops!   19
6 Mistakes Mean . . .   21

FEELINGS

1 Feel Wheel   25
2 We All Have Feelings   27
3 Where Do You Hurt?   29
4 Like 'Em or Not   31
5 Express It!   33
6 I'm Afraid   35

BELIEFS AND BEHAVIOR

1 Fact or Fantasy   39
2 Choosing to Behave   41
3 Sensible or Not Sensible?   43
4 I Have to Have My Way   45
5 Exaggerations   47
6 Cause and Effect   49

PROBLEM SOLVING/DECISION MAKING

1 Decisions and Consequences   53
2 We Can If We Try   55
3 Big and Little Choices   57

4 Multiple Solutions   59

5 What Now?   61

6 Talking It Out   65

INTERPERSONAL RELATIONSHIPS

1 People Sorting   69

2 What's Inside?   71

3 Why Judge?   73

4 Hand Me Some Happiness   75

5 It's OK to Goof Up   77

6 Plus or Minus Tac-Toe   79

Grades 3–4

SELF-ACCEPTANCE

1 Just Different   87

2 Nobody Likes Me   89

3 Put-Downs   91

4 So They Say   93

5 I Can Try   95

6 Perfectly, Perfectly   97

FEELINGS

1 Face Your Feelings   101

2 I Think, I Feel   103

3 How Strong?   105

4 Thermometer of Emotions   107

5 I Feel, I Do   111

6 How Do You Feel?   113

BELIEFS AND BEHAVIOR

1 Facts and Beliefs   117

2 Beliefs, Feelings, and Behaviors   121

3 Checking It Out   123

4 Stop, Go, and Caution   125

5 Options   127

6 It's Awful!   129

PROBLEM SOLVING/DECISION MAKING

1 What Happens When . . .   133

2 Once Upon a Time   135

3 For Better or Worse   137

4 The Ripple Effect   141

5 React and Respond   145

6 R and R   147

INTERPERSONAL RELATIONSHIPS

1 Judgment Machine   151

2 Face the Facts   153

3 Glad to Be Me   155

4 It's Me!   157

5 One of a Kind   161

6 True Blue   165

Grades 5–6

SELF-ACCEPTANCE

1 Who Isn't What?   171

2 I Am, I Do   173

3 Me Power   175

4 Voicebox   177

5 Performance Wheel   179

6 Accept or Change   183

FEELINGS

1 They Made Me Feel   187

2 Help or Hinder?   189

3 Healthy/Unhealthy Expression   191

4 Changing Thoughts, Changing Feelings   193

5 How Might They Feel?   197

6 Feelings and Physical Reactions   199

BELIEFS AND BEHAVIOR

1 Rational or Irrational   203

2 It's Always   207

3 Shoulds, Shoulds, Shoulds   209

4 Rose-Colored Glasses   211

5 Consequences   215

6 Erase the Irrational   217

PROBLEM SOLVING/DECISION MAKING

1 Approach or Avoid   221

2 Assess the Decision   223

3 Yours vs. Mine vs. Ours   225

4 If I Say So   227

5 One Step at a Time   229

6 Goal for It   233

INTERPERSONAL RELATIONSHIPS

1 Choices, Choices Everywhere   237

2 Guessing Game   239

3 One Plus One Plus One   241

4 Say What?   243

5 Solve It   245

6 Tune It   247

Index of Activities   249

About the Author   251

FOREWORD

Albert Ellis claims to have invented Rational-Emotive Therapy (RET) in elementary school as a way to cope with his own feelings about being a latchkey child and to have reinvented it in his early 20s as a means to overcome his intense shyness. Later on, in the 1960s, Ellis began to use RET in his professional practice with individuals and couples. In doing so, he noted two interesting things: First, his sex and marital therapy with couples involved more direct teaching than did his more psychoanalytically oriented individual practice. And, second, his sex and marital therapy clients improved much faster than his individual clients.

Even though RET began as a psychotherapy intended for use with adults, it has always had a psychoeducational emphasis. Not only does RET involve active teaching of principles and ideas, it also can be understood even by young children and readily used outside of the therapeutic setting to overcome emotional problems.

In the present volume and its companion volume for adolescents, Ann Vernon has extended the early work of Ellis and other practitioners of RET to create the most detailed, explicit, and comprehensive lesson plans currently available for teaching RET principles. Importantly, the exercises contained here are based on the results of many research studies into the effects of RET in the educational area. The activities are appropriate for children in regular classes; in addition, they will be especially useful in working with children already identified as having emotional problems.

Finally, research suggests that efforts to help students stay emotionally healthy are best begun long before problems arise. Psychotherapists and counselors working with children and adolescents individually or in groups will no doubt find the activities contained here very helpful. My greatest hope for this volume and its companion, however, is that they will be widely applied in the classroom as a effort toward such primary prevention.

Raymond DiGiuseppe
Institute for Rational-Emotive Therapy

ACKNOWLEDGMENTS

This book and its companion volume, *Thinking, Feeling, Behaving: An Emotional Education Curriculum for Adolescents*, are the result of years of training and practicing Rational-Emotive Therapy (RET). Thanks for the original impetus go naturally to Dr. Albert Ellis, founder of RET and Director of the Institute for Rational-Emotive Therapy.

It was at the Institute where I was first introduced to the concept of rational-emotive education in a presentation by Dr. Virginia Waters. I would like to thank Dr. Waters and also Dr. Richard Wessler, who offered to critique my first efforts to create emotional education activities for young people, collected in *Help Yourself to a Healthier You* (Minneapolis: Burgess, 1989).

With the encouragement of Dr. Ray DiGiuseppe, I undertook further RET training. I would like to thank him for his support, as well as for referring me to Maria Columbo, an elementary school teacher in Canton, Ohio, who collaborated on lesson objectives and contributed activities in the interpersonal relationships and problem-solving/decision-making sections of this volume. My gratitude goes to all of these people for their contributions to a program I think will have a positive influence on the lives of many young people.

INTRODUCTION

We live in a time marked by rapid change. All of us are faced with the challenge of adjusting to a world that is no longer as predictable and secure as it once was, and, for children, growing up is more difficult than ever before. Although many young people are able to master these life challenges, childhood stress is at epidemic proportions—and childhood depression and suicide are also on the increase. These problems make a dramatic statement about how difficult it is for many young people to cope with contemporary issues as well as with the typical milestones that characterize childhood development.

Given these realities, it is imperative that we address the social and emotional development of our children. Parents must necessarily shoulder much of this burden, but schools can also encourage such learning. Our responsibilities as educators and counselors include not only providing young people with knowledge and facts, but also teaching them the survival skills they will need to cope successfully with modern-day living.

An Emotional Health Curriculum

The purpose of this volume and its companion, *Thinking, Feeling, Behaving: An Emotional Education Curriculum for Adolescents,* is to provide educators, counselors, school psychologists, social workers, and others working in the schools with a comprehensive curriculum to help youngsters learn positive mental health concepts. Each volume contains a total of 90 activities, field tested, arranged by grade levels, and grouped into the following topic areas: Self-Acceptance, Feelings, Beliefs and Behavior, Problem Solving/Decision Making, and Interpersonal Relationships.

Several features distinguish this curriculum from other efforts to teach mental health concepts. First, lessons are sequential in nature and developmentally appropriate for the grade levels specified. The two volumes used together thus provide an integrated program for students in grades 1–12. This approach, in which activities for children at different developmental levels build upon previous program experiences, can be expected to have an effect well beyond that of less systematic efforts.

Next, each activity seeks to achieve a specific objective. These objectives, plainly stated, offer guidance in what concepts to stress and what outcomes to expect. In addition, each activity contains both content and personalization discussion questions that may be expanded upon, if desired. Content questions ensure mastery of concepts, whereas personalization questions encourage students to apply the concepts they learn. This personalization component is critical because it helps to move students from intellectualization about what they learn to understanding of how such learning can enable them to cope more positively with the challenges of growing up. Finally, student involvement characterizes all activities, with participants deducing understandings from simulation games, role playing, stories, written activities, brainstorming, and art activities.

Perhaps the most important feature of the curriculum concerns the fact that its

1

content is strongly based on the theoretical principles of Rational-Emotive Therapy (RET), a system uniquely suited to emotional education.

Foundations of Rational-Emotive Therapy

Because only a brief overview is possible here, readers unfamiliar with RET are encouraged to study further the references listed at the end of this introduction. However, the following discussion will attempt to describe briefly the basic premises of the theory.

Based on the work of Albert Ellis, founder of the Institute for Rational-Emotive Therapy in New York, RET is a counseling intervention generally based on the assumption that emotional problems result from faulty thinking about events rather than from events themselves. As such, it involves a cognitive-emotive-behavioral system. This idea is illustrated by the A–B–C theory of emotional disturbance, where A is an activating event, B are beliefs about the event, and C is the emotional and behavioral consequence.

A $\longrightarrow$ B $\longrightarrow$ C
Activating Event   Beliefs   Consequence

Many people feel that activating events cause consequences. However, RET thinking holds that beliefs about the event intervene and are critical in determining consequences. If beliefs are rational, they result in moderate emotions that enable people to act constructively and achieve their goals. In contrast, irrational beliefs lead to disturbed emotions such as anger, anxiety, or depression, thus making goal attainment difficult.

The core construct of RET is that emotional upset stems from three major irrational beliefs.

1. I must do well and win approval for my performances, or else I rate as a rotten person.

2. Others must treat me considerately and kindly in precisely the way I want them to treat me; if they don't, society and the universe should severely blame, damn, and punish them for their inconsiderateness.

3. Conditions under which I live must get arranged so that I get practically everything I want comfortably, quickly, and easily, and get virtually nothing that I don't want. (Ellis, 1980, pp. 5–7)

These irrational beliefs result in some very nonproductive feelings and attitudes.

1. Worthlessness ("I am a worthless person if I don't do as well and win as much approval as I must.")

2. Awfulizing ("It is awful, terrible, or horrible that I am not doing as I must.")

3. I-can't-stand-it-itis ("I can't stand, can't bear the things that are happening to me that must not happen!") (Ellis, 1980, p. 8)

The "must" that characterizes these feelings and attitudes translates into the following kinds of statements, easily recognizable to anyone who works with school-age youngsters.

2

It's awful if others don't like me; I'm bad if I make a mistake; Everything
should go my way and I should always get what I want; Things should come
easily for me; The world should be fair; I must win; I shouldn't have to wait
for anything; It's better to avoid challenges than to risk failure; I must
conform to my peers; I can't stand to be criticized; It's my parents' fault that
I'm miserable; I can't help the way I am. (Waters, 1982, p. 572)

Once such irrational beliefs are identified, the D and E of the A–B–C paradigm become
operative. Disputing (D) means challenging irrational beliefs by questioning assumptions
about the event. As disputing occurs and rational beliefs replace irrational ones, more
moderate emotions (E) result.

To illustrate, take the example of Eric, an 8-year-old who wasn't invited to a
classmate's birthday party. If Eric had been upset (C—emotional consequence) because he
hadn't been invited to the party (A—activating event), he might tell himself that it was
awful that he wasn't invited, that his classmate should have invited him, and that, because
he hadn't been invited, he must be worthless (B—irrational beliefs). In order to help Eric
deal with the problem, we would want to encourage him to challenge these irrational
beliefs by disputation (D). To do so, we might ask the following questions to help Eric put
the problem in perspective and come up with a less intense emotion (E).

1. Just because you didn't get invited to the party, does that mean you're really
   no good?
2. What are some other reasons that you might not have been invited?
3. Suppose that everyone except you did get invited. Does that mean it's so
   awful you can't stand it?
4. Why should your classmate invite you just because you want to go?
5. Since you didn't get invited to the party, how can you handle this situation?

Applications of RET with Young People

In 1970, the Institute for Rational Living opened The Living School, a private grade school
in New York. The purpose of this school was to present RET concepts in addition to the
typical elementary-level curriculum. During the course of the school's operation, it became
evident that teachers could successfully help children improve their emotional health.
Currently, RET is used extensively with children and adolescents, either on an individual
basis, in the classroom, or in small-group counseling sessions.

There are several reasons an emotional education curriculum based on RET principles
can be successful with school-age children. First, RET is educative in nature, its goal being
to help people help themselves by teaching them positive mental health concepts. More
importantly, the core irrational beliefs RET attempts to modify relate to many of the basic
problems faced by young people today: equating self-worth with performance and
therefore never feeling good about oneself; awfulizing about events, then reacting in self-
defeating ways (for example, by abusing alcohol or drugs); overgeneralizing and losing
perspective on problems, then reacting impulsively (perhaps even by committing suicide).
In addition, many young people seem to be caught up in the irrational attitude that things
should come easily; this perspective results in impatience about having to work hard and

3

set long-term goals. Finally, unless young people are taught to change these negative feelings by changing their thoughts, efforts at prevention or remediation will be superficial. A central goal of RET is to help people successfully alter these thoughts.

The activities in this volume address core irrational concepts through a variety of participant activities and deductive questions. For example, Grades 1–2 Self-Acceptance Activity 5 (Oops!) attempts to combat the belief children frequently hold that they are "bad" if they make a mistake. Specifically, children listen to a story about a boy who wrote the words *stupid pig* on his spelling test because he made a mistake. Through a series of questions, children are able to see that the mistake wasn't a major one, that the boy didn't need to put himself down for making it, and that making mistakes and learning from them is natural. Another commonly held irrational belief is that one shouldn't show one's feelings. Grades 5–6 Feelings Activity 3 (Healthy/Unhealthy Expression) uses a worksheet to help children identify appropriate methods of expressing anger, disappointment, fear, worry, and sadness.

Using Program Materials

In recent years, increasing interest has been shown toward developing preventative delivery systems designed to minimize or eliminate potential problems youngsters may experience. As noted by Bernard and Joyce (1984), the goal of preventative mental health programs is to facilitate the social and emotional growth of children by developing interpersonal relationship skills, enhancing self-esteem, improving problem-solving and decision-making strategies, developing a flexible outlook on life, acquiring a personal value system, and learning communication skills. Insofar as is possible, it is recommended that program activities be used in a preventative way, before problems in these areas arise. The program also lends itself to remediative efforts, however, and can be used successfully to intervene with youngsters who are having specific adjustment problems.

Activities are primarily intended to be used in classroom or small-group counseling settings. With minor adaptations, they can also be used in individual counseling sessions. Other adaptations may be required to ensure that activities are appropriate for particular situations and groups; these alterations are encouraged, as is the creation of new activities.

Each activity contains two main parts: a stimulus activity and discussion. At the beginning of the session, it is a good idea to explain the lesson's objective, particularly for older youngsters. Stimulus activities are generally designed to last 15–20 minutes so that, in the confines of the typical class of 30–35 minutes, at least 15 minutes can be devoted to discussion. The discussion will allow students to learn specific skills; be introspective about particular concepts; and gain insights to help them learn more about themselves, their relationships, their behaviors, and their feelings. Since discussion is a critical element of the activities, whenever possible it is a good idea to have students seated in a circle.

Many of the activities encourage students to look at themselves and to share and learn from classmates with regard to emotional adjustment. It is therefore imperative that an atmosphere of trust and group cohesion be established. If the appropriate atmosphere exists, students often welcome the opportunity to share. However, if children seem uncomfortable sharing something personal, allow them to "pass." Don't force them to participate in discussion. Just hearing the other participants share and discuss will be a learning experience and will help normalize feelings and thoughts youngsters may have had but were simply reluctant to bring up.

It is also important that certain ground rules be established early on. Such rules can help to ensure that youngsters respect one another's opinions and expressions, understand that discussion of a personal nature is confidential and should stay within the group, and know that they have a choice whether or not they share personal information about themselves. Consistently enforcing these ground rules will provide children with a "safe space" to express their feelings and will encourage them to feel free to learn these important concepts.

For Further Information

Bernard, M.E., & Joyce, M.R. (1984). *Rational-Emotive Therapy with children and adolescents: Theory, treatment strategies, preventative methods.* New York: Wiley.

Dryden, W., & Trower, P. (Eds.). (1986). *Rational-Emotive Therapy: Recent developments in theory and practice.* Bristol, England: Institute for Rational-Emotive Therapy.

Ellis, A. (1962). *Reason and emotion in psychotherapy.* New York: Lyle Stuart.

Ellis, A. (1971a). *Growth through reason.* North Hollywood, CA: Wilshire.

Ellis, A. (1971b). *Humanistic psychotherapy.* New York: Crown.

Ellis, A. (1980). An overview of the clinical theory of Rational-Emotive Therapy. In R. Grieger & J. Byrd (Eds.), *Rational-Emotive Therapy: A skills-based approach.* New York: Van Nostrand.

Ellis, A., & Bernard, M.E. (1983). *Rational-emotive approaches to the problems of childhood.* New York: Plenum.

Ellis, A., & Grieger, R. (1977). *Handbook of Rational-Emotive Therapy.* New York: Springer.

Ellis, A., & Whitely, J.M. (1979). *Theoretical and empirical foundations of Rational-Emotive Therapy.* Monterey, CA: Brooks/Cole.

Grieger, R., & Boyd, J. (1980). *Rational-Emotive Therapy: A skills-based approach.* New York: Van Nostrand.

Vernon, A. (1983). Rational-emotive education. In A. Ellis & M. Bernard (Eds.), *Rational-emotive approaches to the problems of childhood.* New York: Plenum.

Walen, S.R., DiGiuseppe, R.A., & Wessler, R.L. (1980). *A practitioner's guide to Rational-Emotive Therapy.* New York: Oxford.

Waters, V. (1982). Therapies for children: Rational-Emotive Therapy. In C.R. Reynolds & T.B. Gutkin (Eds.), *Handbook of school psychology.* New York: Wiley.

Wessler, R.A., & Wessler, R.L. (1983). *The principles and practice of Rational-Emotive Therapy.* San Francisco: Jossey-Bass.

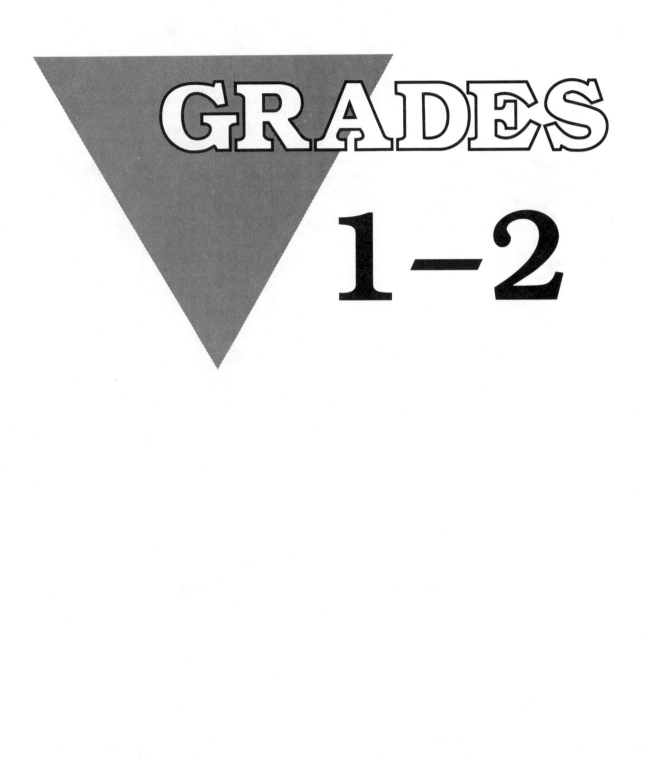

GRADES
1-2

SELF-ACCEPTANCE

People Hunt

Objective

To recognize that there is something unique about everyone

Materials

People Hunt Chart

Procedure

1. Introduce the activity by telling the children that they are going to go on a "people hunt" in order to find out some things about their classmates. Explain that part of the activity will require them to look and listen but not speak.

2. Hold up the People Hunt Chart and read the first four items across. Without speaking, the children are to get up and move around the room slowly, observing their classmates and finding people who have the characteristics described by the four items in the first row.

3. After a short period, call students back. As a group, discuss their findings about the first four items and fill in one or two names per square.

4. Read the four items in the next row, this time asking students to raise their hands if the items apply to them. Record names on the chart.

5. Read the items in the last row. Filling in names for the items in this row will require students to share information about themselves. Fill in the chart with their responses.

Discussion

Content Questions

1. What did you learn about someone else in this class? Share examples.
2. Could everyone's name go into each square on the poster? Why or why not?
3. What does this activity tell us about the people in this class?
4. Do you think that it is good that people are different? Why or why not?

Personalization Questions

1. How are you alike or different from someone else in this group? Share examples.
2. How do you feel about being similar to or different from others?

To the Leader

The important point to emphasize in the discussion is that everyone is unique and that, although there are many ways in which we are like other people, there are also ways in which each of us is different. Help children understand that being different doesn't make one better or worse—just unique.

People Hunt Chart

Directions: Make this chart large enough so that names can be written in as students share.

1	Has brown eyes _____ _____ _____	Has at least one freckle _____ _____ _____	Has a missing tooth _____ _____ _____	Is taller than many kids in class _____ _____ _____
2	Has more than two brothers or sisters _____ _____ _____	Is the youngest in the family _____ _____ _____	Has a grandparent living in this town _____ _____ _____	Has one or more pets _____ _____ _____
3	Lives on the same street as another classmate _____ _____ _____	Can stand on one foot for 10 seconds _____ _____ _____	Has a birthday in the same month as another student _____ _____ _____	Has the same middle name as someone else in the room _____ _____ _____

People Poster

Objective

To learn that people have many different qualities and characteristics

Materials

People Posters (Handout 1); crayons or markers as needed

Procedure

1. Distribute one People Poster (Handout 1) per child. Explain that children will be drawing pictures to illustrate some of the special things that tell about them. Give them about 15 minutes to complete their drawings.

2. Read the information in the first square and ask for several volunteers to share their pictures. Identify each of the responses on the chalkboard. Do the same for the other squares so that you have four lists identifying drawings from each square.

Discussion

Content Questions

1. How many of you could have drawn a picture in the first square like one another classmate drew? (Ask the same question for the other squares.)

2. Look at your People Poster. Can you describe who you are by looking at only one square, or is it better to look at all of them?

Personalization Questions

1. If someone says to you, "Sally, you're a swimmer," is that the only thing you are? What else might you say? Share examples.

2. As you grow older, what do you suppose will happen to you? Do you think your characteristics will change?

To the Leader

It is important to get across the notion that people are made up of different, changing qualities and that we can't identify ourselves in just one way.

People Poster

Something you like to do	Something you don't like to do
Something special about you	**Something you're good at doing**

Can Do, Can't Do

Objective

To learn that people have both strengths and weaknesses

Materials

Can Do, Can't Do Skill Chart

Procedure

1. Explain to the children that you are going to be taking a look at what they can and can't do. Indicate that, when you read an item from the Can Do, Can't Do Skill Chart, they are to stand up if they can do the activity. Point out that there will be some things that they can do and others that they can't. Explain that this is because everyone has strengths in certain areas and not in others.

2. Read the items on the chart and record the names of the children who stand up. After several items have been read, stop and discuss the Content and Personalization Questions. Continue reading the other items on the chart, recording names of those who can do the particular skills.

Discussion

Content Questions

1. When you look at the chart, do you see that there are some things that more students can do than others? Share.
2. Is there anyone who is able to do everything?
3. Is there anyone who isn't able to do anything?

Personalization Questions

1. How do you feel about the things that you can do?
2. What do you think it means if there are things that you can't do?
3. Do you think that there is anyone who can do everything?
4. If you can't do something now, do you think that you might be able to learn to do it sometime during your life?
5. What did you learn about things you can and cannot do?

To the Leader

It is important to emphasize that everyone has strengths and weaknesses and that it is natural to be able to do some things and not others.

Can Do, Can't Do Skill Chart

Directions: Reproduce the chart below on a large sheet of poster paper.

Names

Draw	_____	_____	_____	_____	_____	_____
Write your name	_____	_____	_____	_____	_____	_____
Say ABC's	_____	_____	_____	_____	_____	_____
Drive a car	_____	_____	_____	_____	_____	_____
Ride a horse	_____	_____	_____	_____	_____	_____
Count to 25	_____	_____	_____	_____	_____	_____
Play the piano	_____	_____	_____	_____	_____	_____
Speak another language	_____	_____	_____	_____	_____	_____
Swim a mile at one time	_____	_____	_____	_____	_____	_____

Changes, Changes

Objective

To recognize that people grow and change

Materials

Letter to parent(s); child's object (as described)

Procedure

1. Introduce the activity by explaining that children will each bring an object to school that represents some way in which they have grown or changed since they have been babies. Examples include baby toys, bottles, or infant or toddler clothing.

2. On the day assigned, ask students to share by showing the object and explaining how they are different now from the earlier time (for example, they may not like to play with baby toys anymore, they may not use a bottle, they may wear larger clothing, etc.).

Discussion

Content Questions

1. What are some of the ways in which you have changed? (List these on the chalkboard.)
2. Have you changed in many ways or in just one way?
3. Do you think you will keep on changing as you grow?

Personalization Questions

1. How do you feel about changing as you get older?
2. What are some good things about the changes that have happened to you?
3. What are some of the things that you wish didn't have to change?
4. What is one change that you especially like?

To the Leader

It is important to acknowledge the ambivalence of change, yet stress the fact that we all do grow and change in many different ways.

Sample Letter to Parents

Dear Parent(s):

In guidance class, we are learning about how people grow and change. Could you please help by discussing with your child some way in which he or she has changed since birth and sending an object to school to represent that change? Examples might include an item of clothing that no longer fits, a story that no longer interests them, etc. These items will be needed by [date].

Thank you.

Oops!

Objective

To learn that everyone makes mistakes and that making mistakes is natural

Materials

Story "Oliver Oopsickle Makes a Mistake"

Procedure

1. Introduce the story by explaining that it is about a boy who makes a mistake and how he feels and what he thinks about himself. Read the story, then discuss.

Oliver Oopsickle Makes a Mistake

Oliver Oopsickle was in first grade. His teacher's name was Mr. Warbuckle. One day, Mr. Warbuckle called Oliver in from recess so that he could talk to him. On his way into the building, Oliver thought to himself, "Oops . . . what did I do wrong?"

"Oliver," said Mr. Warbuckle, "please sit down." Oliver was so nervous that he missed the chair and sat on the floor. As he pulled himself up, he thought to himself, "Boy, what a clumsy fool you are, Oliver."

"Oliver, I'm concerned about your spelling paper," said Mr. Warbuckle.

"Oh," said Oliver, "I know. I'm so stupid . . . I missed one word."

"Oliver, that's not what I meant. What bothered me is that you wrote *stupid pig* all over your paper just because you missed one word. Don't you think it's OK to goof up sometimes?"

"Well," said Oliver, "I don't know. I studied my words, and I've never missed any before. I'm mad because I didn't get them all OK."

"I understand, Oliver, but you can't always do things perfectly. We all make mistakes sometimes, no matter how hard we try."

"Oh," said Oliver. "That's news to me. Does that mean I can miss all my words and not be a stupid pig?"

"Well, not exactly," explained Mr. Warbuckle. "It means that it's important to try and do your best, but you can't always do everything right . . . and you're certainly not a stupid pig if you make mistakes. Now you can go back to recess."

Oliver breathed a deep sigh and ran out the door. Suddenly, he turned around. "Oops!" he said. "I forgot my coat. Guess I made a mistake, but that's OK."

Discussion

Content Questions

1. What mistake did Oliver make?
2. Was his mistake a big one or one that anyone could make?
3. What did Oliver learn from his teacher about mistakes?
4. How did Oliver feel about his mistake?

Personalization Questions

1. Have you ever made a mistake? Share examples.
2. How did you feel about the mistake you made?
3. Do you think that it is OK to make mistakes sometimes?
4. Did you learn anything from making your mistake?

To the Leader

It is good to emphasize that one shouldn't try to make mistakes, but that when mistakes happen they aren't terrible or unusual.

Mistakes Mean . . .

Objective

To learn that making mistakes doesn't make people bad or stupid

Materials

Story "Oliver Oopsickle Makes a Mistake" from Grades 1–2 Self-Acceptance Activity 5 (Oops!)

Procedure

1. Introduce the lesson by reviewing the story about Oliver Oopsickle and his mistake. Ask the children if they recall what Oliver wrote on his spelling paper when he knew that he had misspelled a word (*stupid pig*). Discuss the Content Questions.

2. Invite students to share examples of mistakes they have made, then discuss the Personalization Questions.

Discussion

Content Questions

1. Was Oliver a stupid pig just because he misspelled a word?

2. Just because Oliver made a mistake, does that mean he is no good?

3. Did calling himself a stupid pig help Oliver learn to spell better? Do you think it did him any good at all?

Personalization Questions

1. Have you ever felt dumb, stupid, or no good when you've made a mistake? Are you dumb when you make a mistake?

2. What have you learned from Oliver that you can use next time you make a mistake?

To the Leader

Emphasizing the fact that making a mistake does not mean that you are incompetent, bad, or stupid will help students see that they are fallible but still OK.

FEELINGS

Feel Wheel

Objective

To develop a feeling vocabulary

Materials

Feel Wheel

Procedure

1. Introduce the activity by asking children to raise their hands if they have ever felt happy, sad, disappointed, worried, etc. Explain that these feelings are natural and that everyone has feelings like these.

2. Show students the Feel Wheel, explaining that they will be using it in a game. In this game, one person will spin the spinner and, when it lands on a feeling, will try to explain what that feeling means and give an example of a time he or she felt like that. Indicate that, if the spinner lands on the same feeling when the next person spins, the person will spin again so all the words can be discussed.

Discussion

Content Questions

1. Were there any feelings that you had never experienced?

2. Were some of the examples that were shared by other students similar to your experiences when you have had a particular feeling?

Personalization Questions

1. Which feelings do you most like to experience?

2. Which feelings do you least like to experience?

3. What did you learn about your feelings or the feelings of others?

To the Leader

Children at this age might not be able to express clearly what a particular feeling means. To help them, you might ask if the feeling is positive (good) or negative (bad), whether they know another word for the same feeling, whether they can describe it, etc.

Feel Wheel

Directions: Construct the Feel Wheel of posterboard or other heavy paper and use a brass brad in the center to attach the spinner.

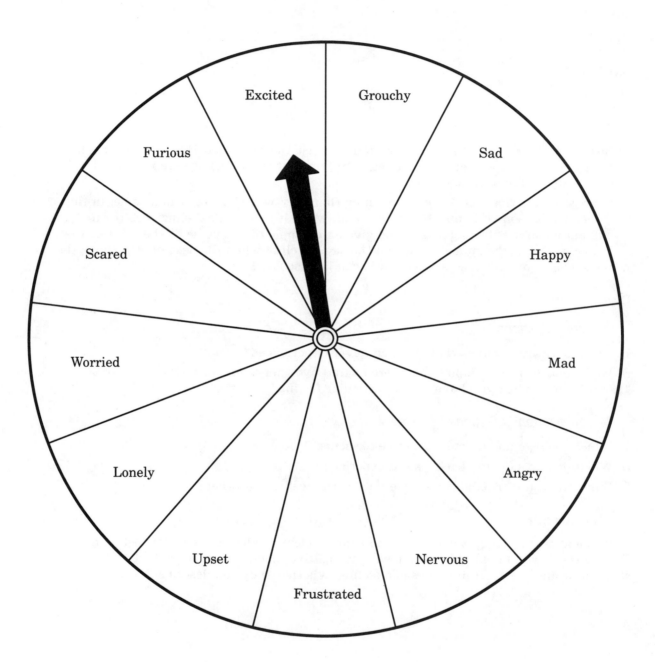

We All Have Feelings

Objective

To learn that it is normal to have feelings

Materials

A stuffed animal; story "Sam's Feelings"

Procedure

1. Begin the activity by holding up the stuffed animal and introducing it as your friend Sam. Explain that you are going to be telling the children a story about your friend and some of the feelings he had when certain things happened to him.
2. Read the story, then discuss.

Sam's Feelings

Sam and his parents were going to the shopping center. On the way there, his parents told him that it was really important for him to stay beside them all the time so that he wouldn't get lost. When they got to the store, his mother told him that, if he stayed close, he could look in the toy department after they had done their shopping.

For a while Sam did stay beside his parents, but he was really bored and started whining about wanting to go home. His parents were busy and just ignored him, so he wandered off alone in search of the toys. Sam thought he knew exactly where he was going, but pretty soon he figured that he was lost. He didn't know what to do. He was getting kind of scared, and he wished he had listened to his mom and dad.

Sam just kept wandering around, but suddenly he heard his mother calling his name. Sam felt so relieved—and so did his parents! But because he had disobeyed them and wandered off, his dad and mom said that he couldn't buy the toy that he had been wanting. He felt angry.

Later that day, Sam thought about the toy that he had wanted and was sad. It would have been fun to have something different to play with. He was upset and decided that the next time he went shopping he would obey his parents.

Discussion

Content Questions

1. What were some of the feelings that Sam and his parents had? (List them on the chalkboard as students recall them.)
2. Can you think of any other feelings Sam might have had in these situations?
3. Based on Sam's experience, do you think that most of us have feelings every day?

Personalization Questions

1. Have you ever experienced feelings like these? Share some examples of what was occurring when you experienced a similar feeling.

2. Share some of the different feelings you've had today.

To the Leader

It is important for children to recognize that they do have feelings in all sorts of situations.

Where Do You Hurt?

Objective

To learn to distinguish between physical and emotional hurt

Materials

One bandaid and one paper heart (with a piece of tape on the back) per child

Procedure

1. Distribute the bandaids and paper hearts, asking children to put them on. Indicate that you will be discussing two kinds of hurt: physical hurt, in which you might use a bandaid, and emotional hurt, in which your feelings are hurt. (Since we associate feelings with our hearts, the hearts might make it easier to remember this difference.)

2. Read the following situations and have children take turns sharing how they might feel and identifying the feeling as a physical hurt or an emotional hurt. (They can do this by pointing to the heart or the bandaid.)

   You are riding your bike and fall and skin your knee. (physical)

   Your pet dies. (emotional/sad)

   Your grandparent is sick. (emotional/worried)

   You are playing in a piano recital. (emotional/nervous)

   You trip on the playground and hurt your arm. (physical)

   Your little sister falls down and is hurt quite badly. (physical for her; emotional/worry for you)

Discussion

Content Questions

1. What do you think is the difference between physical and emotional hurt?
2. Was it difficult for you to distinguish between these two types of hurt? What cues did we use in this activity that might help you remember?

Personalization Questions

1. Which kind of hurt do you experience more often: physical or emotional?
2. Have you ever been in a situation where you have experienced both kinds of hurt at the same time?
3. Next time you have a physical or an emotional hurt, what can you do to make yourself feel better?

To the Leader

This last Personalization Question introduces the important idea that you can do something about your hurt. Through discussion, children can be helped to see that they can talk about the feeling with someone else, get involved in another activity, draw a picture or write a poem or story about the feeling, punch a pillow to vent angry feelings, etc.

Like 'Em or Not

Objective

To learn to differentiate between pleasant and unpleasant feelings

Materials

Feeling Situation Cards

Procedure

1. Introduce the activity by writing the following headings on the chalkboard: *Feelings You Like to Have* and *Feelings You Don't Like to Have*. Give each student a Feeling Situation Card and ask for several volunteers to read and react to the situations.

2. As students individually read the situations, ask them to identify how they might feel in that situation and say whether the feeling is one they like to have (pleasant) or don't like to have (unpleasant). Elaborate a bit on the fact that feelings we like to have are usually happy and associated with good things, whereas feelings we don't like to have are associated with unhappy situations. As each student shares the feeling and categorizes it, list it on the board under the appropriate heading.

3. Invite students to think of additional situations and feelings. Categorize them and list them on the board.

Discussion

Content Questions

1. Was it hard to distinguish between the pleasant and unpleasant feelings?
2. Were there any situations that were labeled pleasant but that you feel are unpleasant? Labeled unpleasant but that you feel are pleasant?

Personalization Questions

1. Which kind of feeling would you rather have, pleasant or unpleasant?
2. What do you think you can do to increase your pleasant feelings?

To the Leader

This activity reinforces feeling vocabulary and helps children recognize both pleasant and unpleasant feelings. It is important to emphasize that pleasant feelings are preferable and that children can have some power over how they feel by telling themselves problems can be solved and, just because they feel bad now, that doesn't mean they will feel that way forever.

Feeling Situation Cards

Directions: Copy each situation on a separate index card.

You lost a tooth.

You learned to read.

Your friend hit you.

You lost a book.

Your parents punished you for lying.

You moved to a new school.

Your grandparents came from out of town to visit.

Your brother or sister is sick.

You lost your jacket.

You had to stay in for recess.

You made a new friend.

You didn't get to go to the movie.

Express It!

Objective

To recognize that it is good to express feelings

Materials

One small paper bag and five individual strips of paper per student; crayons or markers as needed

Procedure

1. Introduce the activity by brainstorming some feeling words and listing these on the chalkboard. Clarify the meaning of any words that are unclear.

2. Distribute the paper bags and strips of paper and explain to the children that sometimes we have feelings about certain situations that we keep to ourselves. This is hiding feelings, just as we could hide something in a paper bag and not let anyone see what's inside. Ask children to think about a time when they might have done this and to write down that feeling on a strip of paper and put it in the bag. (Listing the feeling words on the board will help students with identification and spelling.)

3. Ask children if there are also feelings that they don't hide, but share readily with others. (Usually these are happy feelings.) Ask them to write down some of these feelings on the outside of their bags.

4. Invite children to share examples of feelings that they tend to keep inside, away from others, and examples of feelings that they readily share.

Discussion

Content Questions

1. Do you have more feelings that you keep to yourself or more feelings that you express to others?

2. What do you think would happen if you kept all of your feelings to yourself and never expressed them? (Discuss the negative effects of keeping feelings inside, such as having to solve all of your problems without any help from anyone, worrying about something that you don't need to worry about, getting stomachaches because something is bothering you and you don't let it out, etc.)

Personalization Questions

1. Do you usually feel better or worse when you share your feelings with others?

2. Have you ever had a bigger problem when you haven't expressed your feelings, such as getting a stomachache when something has bothered you or worrying a lot about something when it would have helped to share the worry? Share examples.

3. Do you think it is better to express feelings or keep them inside?

To the Leader

It is important to emphasize the negative effects that occur when feelings are bottled up. Expressing feelings is important, and children need to know that it's OK to do so.

I'm Afraid

Objective

To recognize the difference between real danger and fear, and to discuss ways to deal with fears

Materials

Paper and crayons or markers as needed

Procedure

1. Ask for a volunteer to define what it means to be afraid. Indicate that we all feel afraid sometimes and that different things make us feel afraid. Invite students to draw a picture about something that they are or have been afraid of.

2. Before students share their pictures, point out that some things that we are afraid of are things that can really happen, such as being caught in a fire, being in an accident, getting sick, etc. Other things are fears that we imagine, such as monsters in the dark, bogeymen, etc.

3. As students share their pictures, discuss whether the fear is of something that can really happen or of something imagined. Attach the pictures to the bulletin board under the headings *Real Fear* or *Imagined Fear*.

Discussion

Content Questions

1. What do you think is the difference between real and imaginary fears?

2. Were some of the fears that other children had the same as some that you have had? Share examples.

Personalization Questions

1. Are most of your fears real or imaginary?

2. When you are afraid, what are some things that you can do to be less afraid?

To the Leader

Helping children see the distinction between real and imagined fears may in turn help them see that there really isn't any basis for imagined fears. It is also good for them to see that others have fears too and to share ideas about what to do about these feelings. For instance, children could talk to someone about their fears, put a scary mask on the bedroom door to frighten monsters away, imagine that they put their fears in a box on a high shelf, etc.

BELIEFS AND BEHAVIOR

Fact or Fantasy

Objective

To learn to distinguish between fact and fantasy

Materials

A copy of the story *Cinderella*

Procedure

1. Read the story to the students.
2. Discuss what things in the fairy tale could really happen (such as Cinderella's living with a stepmother, not having nice clothes, etc.). List these on the chalkboard under the heading *Fact*. Then explain that a fantasy is something we might like to have happen but that couldn't really happen. Elicit from the students what the fantasies in the story were (such as having the pumpkin turn into a coach, the mice into horses, etc.). List these on the board under the heading *Fantasy*.

Discussion

Content Questions

1. Was it difficult to tell the difference between what was real and what was fantasy in this fairy tale? What is the difference?
2. Do you think that having fantasies is good?

Personalization Questions

1. Do you ever have a problem distinguishing between what is real and what isn't in your life? For example, have you ever had an imaginary friend that you believed in so much that you thought he or she were real?
2. Have you ever made up stories about things that weren't real, but that you wished were real? For example, have you ever told someone that you had brothers and sisters just because you wanted them, even though you didn't really have them? Do you think that doing this ever becomes a problem?
3. What have you learned about fact and fantasy?

To the Leader

Children of this age often confuse fact and fantasy. Although doing so is not altogether bad, it is far healthier for children to acknowledge what is fact and deal with it directly. The point of this lesson is not to discourage fantasy entirely, but to help students recognize how it differs from fact.

Choosing to Behave

Objective

To recognize that there are many different ways of behaving and that one's behavior is a choice

Materials

None

Procedure

1. Ask students if they know what robots are. Discuss the fact that robots don't really think for themselves, but do what others program them to do. Ask for five volunteers to pretend to be robots. On your command, the robots are to do the following while other students act as observers to see if all robots behave in the same way:

   Stand up.

   Walk slowly.

   Demonstrate what a poor sport acts like.

   Sit down and clown around.

2. Discuss what observers noted and ask for five more volunteers, who are to do the following:

   Demonstrate "good student" behavior.

   Act polite and friendly to an observer.

   Throw a fit.

   Lose your temper.

Discussion

Content Questions

1. Did these robots have much choice about their behavior? Why or why not?
2. Do you think people have a choice about their behavior, or do they have to act the way someone tells them to?
3. Did all of the robots act the same way when asked to do something? What are some of the different behaviors the robots showed?

Personalization Questions

1. Can you think of a time when someone has told you how to behave and you haven't done it? Does this mean that you have a choice about what you do?
2. If you have a choice about how to behave, what are the kinds of behaviors that are better for you and for others?

To the Leader

Emphasizing the fact that children can choose how they behave is important. Even though adults may set rules, children do have the choice whether or not to follow them. Encouraging them to assess behaviors that are better for themselves and others will help them to make appropriate behavioral choices.

Sensible or Not Sensible?

Objective

To help children differentiate sensible expressions of behavior from expressions that are not sensible

Materials

Story "Sensible or Not Sensible"

Procedure

1. Read the story, then discuss.

Sensible or Not Sensible

Nancy (age 6) and Nathan (age 7) were at the supermarket with their dad, who had explained to them that they were to walk quietly through the aisles and not pick up food or knock things off the shelves. If they were good, he said, they could get a treat. As the three of them walked down aisle one, Nancy saw a clerk giving away samples of pizza. Boy, did that look good! She pushed Nathan out of the way and wormed her way up to the front of the line where the lady was passing out bites of pizza. Nathan also wanted a piece, but he stood in line and waited for his. Nancy's dad scolded her and warned her about her behavior.

Down aisle two they went. Nancy and Nathan were getting bored. Nathan stopped to grab some cereal he wanted and ran to the cart to put it in. Dad said to put it back because they didn't need cereal, and Nathan whined, "You never let us eat anything we like."

While Nathan was complaining, Nancy had run ahead and had disappeared into the toy section. Dad asked Nathan to find her because he didn't want them to wander off. Nathan raced down the aisle, almost knocking into an older lady's cart. Halfway down the next aisle, he yelled loudly for Nancy. Nancy ran back and whined to her father that she wanted to go home. Once again, their dad warned them to shape up.

In the next aisle, their dad asked them to pick out potato chips and cookies. They quickly agreed on barbecue chips, and Nancy carried them to the cart. She told Nathan he could choose the cookies. They helped with the rest of the list.

Finally, they got to the checkout counter. Nathan wanted two candy bars and started pouting when his dad said he could only have one. Nancy wanted gum and remembered to say thanks. On the way home, they fought over who could sit in the front seat. They were both assigned to the back seat as they left the supermarket parking lot.

Discussion

Content Questions

1. How did Nancy and Nathan behave in the story? List some of the behaviors they demonstrated.
2. Of these behaviors, which do you think were sensible (appropriate, good) ways to behave? Make a list.
3. Of these behaviors, which do you think were not sensible (inappropriate, bad) ways to behave? Make a list.

Personalization Questions

1. Do you usually behave sensibly or not sensibly?
2. Are you proud of the way you behave?
3. If you aren't proud about your behavior, what can you do about it?
4. Would you like to behave sensibly or not sensibly most of the time? Whom does it hurt if you don't behave sensibly?

To the Leader

If children are able to distinguish between behavior that is sensible and not sensible, they will be more likely to see that they can choose behavior that is in their own best interests.

I Have to Have My Way

Objective

To explore the negative effects of being demanding

Materials

Story "Sid and the Baseball Game"

Procedure

1. Read the story, then discuss.

Sid and the Baseball Game

Sid sat on the curb, waiting for the rest of the kids to come and play ball. When Sally came, she said she'd bat first. Sid stamped his foot on the ground and whined, "I won't play if I can't be first." So the kids let Sid bat first.

The first ball Sid hit was a foul, and so was the next one. Sid yelled that the umpire was cheating and if his foul ball didn't get counted as a run he'd quit. But by this time the kids all said, "OK, quit."

So, as Sid walked away, he yelled, "You'll be sorry. I don't ever want to play with cheaters again." None of the kids responded. They were having a great time and were glad to have someone like Sid out of the game.

Discussion

Content Questions

1. What do you think about Sid's behavior? (Discuss the fact that much of Sid's behavior was demanding that things be the way he wanted them to be.)
2. What does the word *demanding* mean?
3. What were some of the demands that Sid made?
4. What was the result of Sid's demanding? Did it make him happy? How did the others respond?

Personalization Questions

1. Have you ever acted like Sid? Share some examples of times that you have been demanding. Do you like acting in a demanding way?
2. Do you think people should have their way all of the time? If you are demanding, you probably think that you should have your way. Is this possible?
3. Next time you find yourself beginning to demand, what can you do instead?

To the Leader

Demanding has negative payoffs, and students need to realize that they don't have to be demanding. Although it is difficult for youngsters to do, they can stop and ask themselves, "Is it possible for me to always have my way?" "Is it so awful if I don't get exactly what I want?" and "Can't I just accept things the way they are?" Changing children's thinking is a way of altering their demanding behavior.

Exaggerations

Objective

To identify examples and effects of exaggerated thinking

Materials

None

Procedure

1. Discuss with students what it means to exaggerate and give some examples of exaggeration. For instance, "I was walking to school this morning and saw a fight" is not an exaggeration, but "I was walking to school and saw the worst fight I have ever seen—I was sure that the people would kill each other" is probably an exaggeration. Another example of an exaggeration would be "My parents are absolutely the meanest people in the world, and they never let me do anything fun." Discuss the fact that sometimes exaggerations are just things that we think to ourselves and sometimes they are stories that we tell others.

2. Invite students to share some examples of exaggerations.

Discussion

Content Questions

1. What does it mean to exaggerate?
2. What purpose does exaggeration serve? Why do you think people do it?

Personalization Questions

1. If you have ever exaggerated, why have you done it?
2. Do you think that exaggerated thinking has been helpful to you? Is exaggerated thinking ever harmful? (Discuss some of the negative effects, such as having people not believe what you say.)
3. What can you do to stop exaggerated thinking or telling exaggerated stories?

To the Leader

People sometimes exaggerate to make themselves feel more important or to get attention. If children can learn to recognize exaggeration, they may be better able to avoid it.

Cause and Effect

Objective

To recognize cause and effect with regard to behavior

Materials

A straight pin and a blown-up balloon; two puppets; Cause and Effect Situation Cards; a large envelope

Procedure

1. Explain to students that they will be looking at situations in which, because someone does something, something else happens. This is called cause and effect. Show students the pin and the balloon and ask what they think will happen if you poke the balloon with the pin. Ask for a volunteer to poke the balloon; discuss the effect.

2. Call for two volunteers to use the puppets. Ask one child to draw one of the Cause and Effect Situation Cards from the envelope and to follow the instructions. Ask for two more volunteers and follow the same procedure. Repeat until all the situations have been used.

Discussion

Content Questions

1. In each of the situations, did the second puppet do something after the first puppet did? What are some examples of the behaviors that resulted from the first puppet's actions?

2. Do you think the second puppet would have acted the way it did if the first one hadn't done what it did? (Explain again that this process is called cause and effect and simply means that, when someone behaves a certain way, something happens as a result of that behavior.)

Personalization Questions

1. Have you had any experiences similar to the ones illustrated by the puppets?

2. What do the words *cause and effect* mean to you?

To the Leader

Although the relationship between cause and effect is a sophisticated concept, children can begin to see that behavior does have consequences that need to be taken into consideration.

Cause and Effect Situation Cards

Directions: Copy each situation on a separate index card.

First puppet: You are a student. You stick your tongue out at your teacher.
Second puppet: You are the teacher. How will you react to what the first puppet did?

First puppet: You stick your hand in an unfriendly dog's mouth.
Second puppet: You are the dog. What will you do?

First puppet: You don't look both ways when crossing the street.
Second puppet: You are the car. What do you do?

First puppet: You have been called three times to supper, and you finally wander in.
Second puppet: You are the parent. What do you do?

First puppet: You have been told never to open the door and let a stranger in, but you do.
Second puppet: You are the stranger. What might you do?

PROBLEM SOLVING/
DECISION MAKING

Decisions and Consequences

Objective

To learn that there are consequences for the decisions we make

Materials

An egg and bowl; glass of water; birthday candle; Cause Lottery Tickets; paper and crayons or markers as needed

Procedure

1. Demonstrate the cause-effect relationship by dropping an egg into a bowl to make it break, tipping over a glass of water to make it spill, and blowing on a lit birthday candle to extinguish it.

2. Discuss the principle of cause and effect, using the Content Questions.

3. Elicit probable effects for each of the following causes:

    Someone is nice to you.

    Someone tells a funny joke.

    Someone calls you a name.

4. Explain that people's behaviors have causes and effects just like those demonstrated by the egg, water, and candle.

5. Direct a comparison of the following examples to establish that some causes are chosen, whereas others are not. Stress the idea that sometimes we can control effects by choosing causes.

    Cause (not chosen): Someone trips and falls.
    (*cause*)   (*effect*)

    Cause (chosen): Someone tries hard in school and gets a good report card.
    (*cause*)   (*effect*)

6. Have the students give examples of causes we choose that have good effects. These might include sharing with friends, expressing feelings, completing tasks, and so forth. Contrast each positive example with an alternate cause that would have bad effects. Reinforce the connection between cause and effect.

7. Have students fold a sheet of paper in half and label one side *Cause* and the other *Effect*. Then ask students to select a Cause Lottery Ticket. Each student illustrates the idea given on his or her ticket by drawing a picture on the cause half of the paper, then draws another picture on the other half to illustrate the probable effect.

8. Share cause-effect pictures upon completion and discuss Personalization Questions.

Discussion

Content Questions

1. What does any action do? (causes something else to happen)

2. What do people's actions do? (cause something else to happen; cause other people to react)

3. Do we have choices about how we behave?

4. Can we cause good things to happen instead of bad by the choices we make?

Personalization Questions

1. Have you ever done anything that caused something good to happen? Something bad?

2. Can you think of something to do to cause a good thing to happen today? Plan it. Do it and see if it works. (Follow up on students' experiences.)

To the Leader

The relationship of cause and effect is visible around children every day. This lesson can be easily reinforced by paying attention to daily classroom interactions. Remind the students of the cause and effect principle as often as possible, especially in conflict situations, in which children have a tendency not to see how their own behavior has affected others.

Cause Lottery Tickets

Directions: Copy the following statements onto separate index cards.

Cause: Someone is mean to you.

Cause: You disobey the teacher.

Cause: Someone shares with you.

Cause: You say kind things to someone.

Cause: Someone eats too much candy.

Cause: You go to bed too late.

Cause: Someone writes on your desk with marker.

Cause: Someone is playing with matches.

Cause: You help set the table.

Cause: You clean up your room without being told.

Cause: You forget to feed your pets.

Cause: You go outside in cold weather without a coat.

Cause: You get up late.

Cause: You forget to do your homework.

Cause: You don't wear your watch and get home late from a friend's house.

Cause: Someone calls you a name.

Cause: Someone writes on the bathroom wall at school.

Cause: You forget your lunchbox.

Cause: You don't do your chores.

Cause: You tease your baby sister.

We Can If We Try

Objective

To assess the advantages and disadvantages of cooperative and uncooperative decision making

Materials

Sturdy medium-sized wooden box; beanbag; two large stars cut from gold construction paper

Procedure

1. Organize children into three small groups. (Group 1 should contain no more than 5–6 students.)

2. Assign one group to each of the following tasks:

   Group 1 must balance themselves on top of a medium-sized wooden box. At least one foot must be in contact with the box. The other foot may remain in contact with the floor, but no other body parts may do so. The group must be able to remain balanced in that position for at least 10 seconds.

   Group 2 must pass a beanbag relay style from one end of the room to the other without using their hands.

   Group 3 must form a human chain from one gold star placed on the floor to a second gold star placed a distance away. (The distance between the two points should be greater than the distance the students could reach by joining hand to hand at arm's length.)

3. Upon completion of each activity, discuss how each group arrived at a solution to the problem.

Discussion

Content Questions

1. How did your group work together to solve the problem? (Elicit both successful and unsuccessful strategies from each group.)

2. What things worked best in solving the group problems?

3. What kinds of things made it difficult to work out a solution? (Examples might include everyone's talking at once, people's refusing to participate, arguing.)

Personalization Questions

1. How did you feel when the group used one of your ideas? When they did not?

2. In order to solve the problem, what did you have to do when your idea didn't work or wasn't accepted by the group?

3. What did you learn by doing this activity that might help you the next time you work in a group?

To the Leader

It is highly recommended that students be included in group problem solving and decision making in the classroom (for example, planning class activities, addressing specific problems that arise in learning and behavior, and setting class goals).

Big and Little Choices

Objective

To learn to distinguish between major and minor problems and to recognize that these perceptions can change

Materials

Magazine pictures of people in different situations; a large piece of posterboard for each two students; crayons or markers as needed

Procedure

1. Display a variety of magazine pictures showing people in each of the following situations: grocery shopping, reading the classified ads, looking at a new house to buy, and trying on some new shoes.

2. Discuss each picture and identify the decisions connected with the pictures: selecting food to eat, a new job, a new house, a new pair of shoes.

3. Categorize each decision as being either major (big) or minor (little) and explain that one determines whether a decision is major or minor by considering the consequences of the decision (what the long-term effects will be, whether the decision will mean big changes in one's life, etc.).

4. Illustrate that, regardless of whether a decision is major or minor, the decision-making process follows the same steps: gathering information, identifying alternatives, and understanding consequences. For example, in deciding what shoes to buy (a minor decision), you first need to know where you can get shoes. Then you need to look at all the styles, colors, and prices. What happens if you select a black pair instead of brown? Hightops instead of lowcuts? In deciding whether or not to buy a new house (a major decision), a parent would need to know what houses are available and where, as well as how much they cost and how much money the family can afford to spend. What are the neighborhoods like? How will it affect the family to move? Is moving something the family really wants to do?

5. Have students select a partner and together create a display chart of big and little decisions, using additional magazine pictures.

6. Direct sharing of completed charts.

Discussion

Content Questions

1. What is the difference between a big (major) decision and a little (minor) one?

2. Can the same decision be a big one for one person and a small one for another person? (An example would be a teenager's choosing a new after-school job and a parent's choosing a new job to help support a family.)

3. What makes a decision major or minor?

Personalization Questions

1. Has anyone in your family ever made a major decision? What was it? How did it affect your family?
2. What kinds of decisions do you usually make?
3. Why is making good minor decisions important practice for you?

To the Leader

Children often minimize the importance of their decision making because they know their decisions are most often minor ones. It is necessary to develop children's sense of their own power and pride in making even small decisions. Furthermore, it may be helpful to remind children that effective decision-making skills are learned and, as such, require practice that can be provided by making good minor decisions on a daily basis.

Multiple Solutions

Objective

To learn that most problems have more than one solution

Materials

Multiple Solutions Overhead Transparency (Handout 2); paper and crayons or markers as needed

Procedure

1. Project the transparency of various campout food items (Handout 2) on an overhead screen. Direct the children to pick out any four items to pack and draw or list them. Instruct them that they may spend no more than three dollars.
2. Briefly allow children to share selections made, emphasizing that not everyone selected the same items and that there are often many different ways to solve problems.
3. Assign each student to a small group (4–6 students).
4. Direct each small group to solve the following problems, which have been written on the chalkboard:

   The boy next to you in school keeps copying off your paper.

   You are out of milk and want to have cereal for breakfast.

   Your little brother keeps getting into your sticker book when you aren't home.

5. Invite students to share solutions.

Discussion

Content Questions

1. Is there only one solution to a problem, or are there often many different solutions?
2. Were all the different solutions to the problems equally as good? Why were there differences?
3. Why is it sometimes helpful to listen to other people's ideas on how to solve a problem?

Personalization Questions

1. What kinds of problems do you have to solve?
2. Are your solutions ever different from your parents'? Your brothers' or sisters'? Your friends'?
3. What have you learned about solutions to problems?

To the Leader

It is important to encourage children to be open-minded in looking for solutions to everyday problems.

Multiple Solutions Overhead Transparency

SKIPPO Peanut Butter — Original
80¢

WONDER
60¢

SNAKO Potato Chips
95¢

5¢ each

CORNY FLAKES
50¢

ARMY HOT DOGS
75¢

KOOL AID — 10¢ each

Quako OATMEAL — 60¢

What Now?

Objective

To recognize that some problems don't have good solutions

Materials

What Now Game Board and Problem Cards

Procedure

1. Initiate the activity by asking students to raise their hands if they've ever had a problem with no good solution. Share an example, such as when divorced parents both want the child to spend Christmas vacation with them.
2. Indicate that, although there may not be an ideal solution, there usually is a way to work things out.
3. Assign students to small groups (4–6 students). Each small group should be gathered around the What Now Game Board. The first group spins and draws a Problem Card. Children read the card aloud if they are able to; otherwise, the leader may do so. After the card is read, the group comes up with a solution, which they share with the rest of the class.
4. The other groups then spin, select a Problem Card, discuss the solution, and share with the class. (If the problem has already been discussed, the group spins again.)

Discussion

Content Questions

1. What made each of the problem situations so difficult?
2. Are people's needs and desires sometimes impossible for their friends and family to fulfill?
3. Is it anyone's fault that there are problems without good solutions?

Personalization Questions

1. Have you ever had a problem with no good solution?
2. How do you feel when, no matter what you choose to do, your choice is going to hurt someone's feelings?
3. When you have a problem with no good solution, what can you do?
4. Is doing the best you can an acceptable thing to do in a situation with no good solution?

To the Leader

This lesson will require gentle persuasion in addition to explanation and development. Children's keen sense of what is fair and unfair makes it difficult for them to accept realities such as no-win situations. They will not easily be convinced that it's OK only to do the best you can sometimes. It is essential that the leader provide clear, consistent, unwavering affirmation of the fact that it is indeed OK to get caught in such problematic webs and to do the best you can.

What Now Game Board

Directions: Construct the game board of posterboard or other heavy paper. Use a brass brad in the center to attach the spinner.

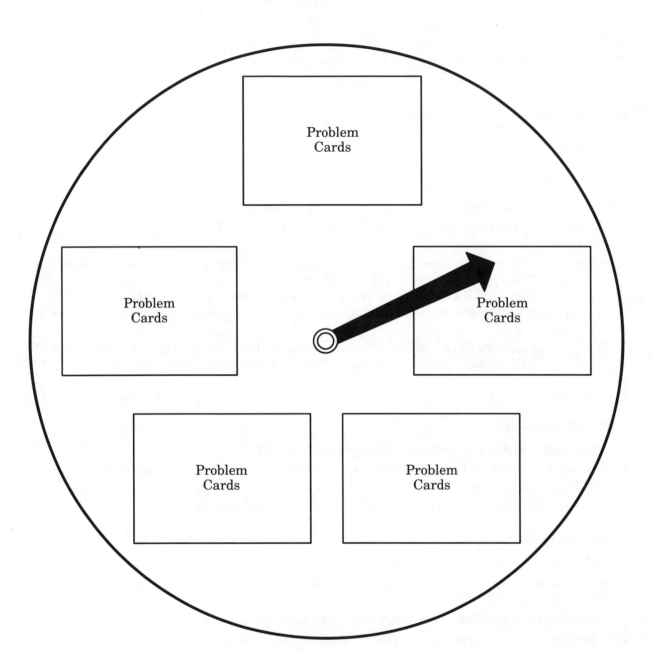

What Now Problem Cards

Directions: Copy the following situations onto separate index cards. Distribute two cards in each space on the game board.

You are accused of cheating on a test because all your answers are the same as your best friend's, who sits next to you. Really, your friend copies off of you without your permission.

Your mom and dad have been fighting a lot lately. Both of them are very unhappy. Your grandma is very worried but doesn't know what's going on. She thinks someone is sick or something. She asks you lots of questions. You know you're not supposed to discuss the situation.

Your parents are separated, and you're afraid they'll get a divorce. You feel really upset, but you're scared to let your parents know because that will make them more upset. Still, you need someone to talk to.

Your dad has been away from home a lot and, when he does come home, he usually drinks a whole lot. He sometimes yells and threatens to hit you. You're scared.

You have stomachaches a lot. Sometimes you call home, and your mom or dad comes to get you and take you to the doctor. But now you're worried because, when you asked your mom if you could go to a movie, she said there wasn't enough money. You feel guilty about being sick and having to spend money for the doctor.

You can only invite six kids to your birthday party. There are nine you'd like to have. How do you choose?

You are invited to an overnight party, but you're afraid to go because sometimes you wet the bed. If you did that at the overnight party, you'd be embarrassed.

Your dog dies. You are very sad and spend all of your time thinking about him and wishing he were alive.

Your best friend is moving away because his dad and mom both lost their jobs. You're really upset that he's moving. Because you think about it so much, your grades are getting worse.

You know that you should always tell the truth, but you don't know what to do now. You saw your older sister take money out of your mom's purse. If you tell, your sister will get mad, but you know that stealing is wrong.

Talking It Out

Objective

To recognize the value in sharing problems with others

Materials

Tape recorders and audiotapes (one recorder and tape for each five students); paper and pencils as needed

Procedure

1. Prior to the lesson, invite students to write down a problem they're experiencing (if students cannot write, they can dictate their problems to the leader). Record these problems on the audiotapes so that there are several problems per tape. Leave ample time between problems for students to record solutions.

2. During the lesson, divide students into groups of five, explaining that they will listen to a problem a student their own age has. After the group listens to the first problem, have one student from the group record a possible solution. (Demonstrate how to use the tape recorder, if necessary.)

3. Once the solution is recorded, group members can discuss other solutions to the problem. They then move on to the next problem recorded on the tape, having another student in the group provide the solution. Continue until all group members have given a solution.

4. Discuss the Content and Personalization Questions with the entire group.

Discussion

Content Questions

1. Were the problems you heard similar to problems you've experienced?
2. Did you think the solutions were good?
3. Have you tried these solutions before for similar problems?
4. Do you think it's better to tell someone else your problem and have him or her help solve it or try to solve problems all by yourself?

Personalization Questions

1. When you have a problem, do you usually talk it out or hold it inside? Which way do you think is best?
2. What did you learn from this activity?

To the Leader

If desired, students' audiotaped solutions can be played back in the larger group for general discussion.

INTERPERSONAL
RELATIONSHIPS

People Sorting

Objective

To identify ways in which people are alike and different

Materials

Old magazines; large-size mural paper; scissors and glue as needed

Procedure

1. Have students make a collection of 6–8 photographs of different kinds of people by cutting pictures from old magazines.
2. Direct an analysis of pictures collected, having children hold up appropriate pictures in response to cues such as the following: someone with blonde hair, someone with blue eyes, someone who looks happy, someone young/old, someone doing work, someone playing.
3. List each of the following four categories on the chalkboard: *Looks*, *Age*, *Feelings*, and *Actions*. Discuss ways people are alike and different across all four categories.
4. Copy the categories onto the mural paper and have children paste their magazine pictures in an appropriate category, printing underneath one or two descriptive words (such as *short*, *young*, *happy*, etc.) corresponding to the category in which the picture is placed.

Discussion

Content Questions

1. Were the people in your pictures all alike? Were they different in some ways?
2. Is it possible to be like other people in some ways and different in other ways? For example, can two people look alike but have different feelings inside them?
3. Are there any ways you can think of that people are alike and different other than the four ways we listed?

Personalization Questions

1. Are you like someone you know in some way? How?
2. Are you different from someone you know in some way? How?
3. Is it wrong to be different from someone else?
4. How does being alike in some ways make people happy?
5. How does being different in some ways make people happy?

To the Leader

It is important to develop the concept that people are alike yet different from one another in more than one dimension. Children often focus only on similarities and differences in physical appearance and need to be invited to consider other aspects of the person.

What's Inside?

Objective

To recognize the effects of labels on relationships

Materials

6–8 tin cans with labels removed; two sets of homemade labels with funny names that will appeal to children and attract their attention, such as *Pete's Pickled Prunes, Henry's Honey Nut Cereal,* and *Sarah's Super Soup*

Procedure

1. Arrange a display of 6–8 cans of similar size and shape with original labels removed and homemade labels applied. The labels should vary in terms of the desirability and appeal of the contents. For example, one can may be labeled *Charlie's Chocolate Fudge Icing* and the next *Pete's Pickled Prunes*.
2. Show each can to the children and read the label aloud.
3. Have the children place bids on the cans according to how much they would be willing to pay for each. Copy the highest bid taken for each on a small price tag and affix to the top of the can.
4. Remove all labels and reapply a second set, altering which cans receive appealing labels as opposed to repulsive ones. Read each label aloud. (Place the original labels under the corresponding cans.)
5. Take bids a second time and copy onto another price tag in a different color ink.

Discussion

Content Questions

1. Why did you bid higher on the cans with labels for good-tasting foods?
2. Did changing the label on the can change what was really inside?
3. Do we really know what is inside these cans?
4. What did changing the labels make us do in our minds?

Personalization Questions

1. Sometimes we label people just like we do cans. We might call them *dumb* or *sweet* or *cute*. Has anyone ever labeled you? Was this label true?
2. How did you feel about that label? Act? How did others act towards you?
3. Do you think labels or names we call people really tell us about what's inside?
4. Do you think those kinds of labels help anyone? Hurt anyone? How?

To the Leader

Children will need careful guidance to make the association between labels on the cans and labels we place on people. The arbitrary nature of the labeling process should be pointed out. Students should continue their discussion until it is clearly established that labels often do not tell us much, can wrongly change our opinion and our valuing of what's inside a person, and are often hurtful.

Why Judge?

Objective

To develop tolerance for others who do not act as we personally prefer them to

Materials

None

Procedure

1. Review the four categories in which people may be alike or different, as developed in Interpersonal Relationships Activity 1 for Grades 1–2 (People Sorting): looks, age, feelings, and actions.
2. Discuss ways in which some people's actions may be different from others' (for example, what people wear, eat, like to do for fun, etc.).
3. Conduct a mock trial in which the group leader plays the attorney and the class play the judge, jury, and defendants. (Select the more self-assured, verbal students to play the defendants.)
4. Enact the trials for the crime scenarios described below and conduct a follow-up discussion for each.

    A person is accused of wearing bright orange socks, which are very ugly.

    A person is accused of not being friendly, happy, and talkative in the early morning.

    A person is accused of not liking the class's favorite food (lima beans).

Discussion

Content Questions

1. Why would a law such as the one this person is accused of breaking be a silly law to have?
2. Does it hurt a person if others behave in ways different from the way he or she might prefer?
3. Instead of laws to protect us from being upset, what do we need to have inside us that will help? (Elicit a definition of tolerance in the children's own language.)

Personalization Questions

1. Have you ever been made fun of or criticized for acting in a way that didn't hurt anyone but that someone else just didn't like? Share examples.
2. How would you feel if we had laws that made us act the exact same way as everyone else all the time?
3. If you wish to be allowed to act the way you are happiest acting, what must you do when others act the way they are happiest acting?

To the Leader

A careful distinction will need to be made between actions that are different and simply not to our liking and actions that are harmful to others and thereby inappropriate. Stressing the absurdity of the sample scenarios and making a point of asking in each case if that behavior really hurts anyone else will help.

Hand Me Some Happiness

Objective

To develop the ability to give and receive compliments

Materials

Assorted colored construction paper; pencils and scissors as needed

Procedure

1. Discuss what a compliment is and how you feel when you give or receive one.
2. Brainstorm and list what kinds of things people give compliments to each other about besides just appearance. List these on the chalkboard.
3. Have each child trace his or her own handprint on colored construction paper, then cut out.
4. Allow students to circulate around the class and select any five children to give a compliment to. When they give the compliment, they are to write it on one of the fingers of the receiving child's cutout hand.
5. Children can wear their cutout hands the remainder of the day.

Discussion

Content Questions

1. How did you feel when you gave a compliment to someone?
2. How did you feel when someone gave you a compliment?
3. How can compliments affect our behavior?

Personalization Questions

1. Do you think the compliments you received today are true?
2. Is it OK to feel good about yourself and the good things you do? How is feeling this way different from bragging?

To the Leader

This activity will need to be closely monitored while compliments are being given and received to assure that children are being sincere and that all children are receiving compliments. Children should be encouraged to remember the different kinds of things about a person to give compliments on besides appearance.

It's OK to Goof Up

Objective

To learn to accept that others can make mistakes

Materials

Pictures of the *Peanuts* character Charlie Brown; OK Kid Badges (Handout 3)

Procedure

1. Select pictures of Charlie Brown in each of his two classic dilemmas: falling flat after attempting to kick a football, which Lucy pulls out from under him, and hanging upside down from a tree limb, entangled in his own kite string. Project the pictures on an opaque projector.
2. Direct a discussion of Charlie Brown's making a mistake, using the Content Questions.
3. Assign each student a partner and instruct pairs to share a personal experience about a time each one made a mistake.
4. After listening to each other's mistake stories, each child comes and gets an OK Kid Badge (Handout 3) and gives it to his or her partner as a sign of acceptance.
5. Children may wear the OK Kid Badges for the remainder of the day.

Discussion

Content Questions

1. Was Charlie Brown a bad person for making mistakes like the ones shown in the pictures?
2. How did Lucy treat Charlie Brown when he made a mistake? Do you think that was the best way to react? Why or why not?

Personalization Questions

1. When your partner told you about his or her mistake, did you feel as though it were a mistake you could have made too?
2. How did you feel when your partner gave you your badge to show you it was OK to make mistakes?

To the Leader

The symbolism of giving the badge as a sign of acceptance and affirmation will need to be fully explained in order for the activity to be effective. Children will need to be encouraged to be sincere in giving the badges and to remain aware of the meaning of what they are doing.

OK Kid Badge

Directions: The group leader can duplicate the badge on colored construction paper and cut out. (Alternatively, children can cut out and color the badges themselves.)

Plus or Minus Tac-Toe

Objective

To learn to distinguish between positive and negative behaviors in interpersonal relationships

Materials

Plus or Minus Tac-Toe Game Cards (Handout 4); crayons or colored markers as needed

Procedure

1. Discuss what plus and minus signs mean.
2. Brainstorm and list examples of plus behaviors, which add to our happiness with others, and minus behaviors, which take away from our happiness with others. (Examples of plus behaviors include smiling, giving compliments, being friendly. Minus behaviors include name-calling, arguing, etc.)
3. Give each student a Plus or Minus Tac-Toe Game Card (Handout 4) and a crayon or colored marker. Explain the rules of the game (as follows).
4. To play, randomly call out the behaviors written on the game cards. (The leader will need a copy of each card.) Students who have a behavior listed on their cards will mark a plus or minus over it when it is called, as appropriate. When a child has three pluses or three minuses lined up in any given row, that child raises his or her hand and calls out, "Plus Tac-Toe" or "Minus Tac-Toe." (There will be multiple, simultaneous winners depending on the number of different cards in play.)

Discussion

Content Questions

1. What is the main difference between plus behaviors and minus behaviors?
2. Which kinds of behaviors do we want to try to engage in more often? Why?

Personalization Questions

1. Think of a plus behavior someone did to you today. How did you feel when this happened? How did you respond?
2. Think of a minus behavior someone did to you today. How did you feel? Respond?
3. Share a plus or minus behavior that you did to someone recently.

To the Leader

Handout 4 provides four different game cards. Depending on the size of the group, others may need to be constructed to avoid too many multiple winners.

Plus or Minus Tac-Toe Game Cards

Smiles at You	Teases You	Ignores You
Calls You a Name	Trips You	Gives You a Hug
Laughs at You	Talks to You	Talks about You

Gives You a Hug	Pushes You	Helps You
Shares with You	Smiles at You	Tattles on You
Tells You a Joke	Cuts in Front of You	Plays with You

Plus or Minus Tac-Toe Game Cards

Hugs You	Smiles at You	Plays with You
Laughs at a Joke You Tell	Teases You	Listens to You
Gives You a Present	Frowns at You	Lies to You

Smiles at You	Sticks Out Their Tongue at You	Teases You
Tells You a Secret	Pinches You	Bites You
Gives You a Present	Frowns at You	Lies to You

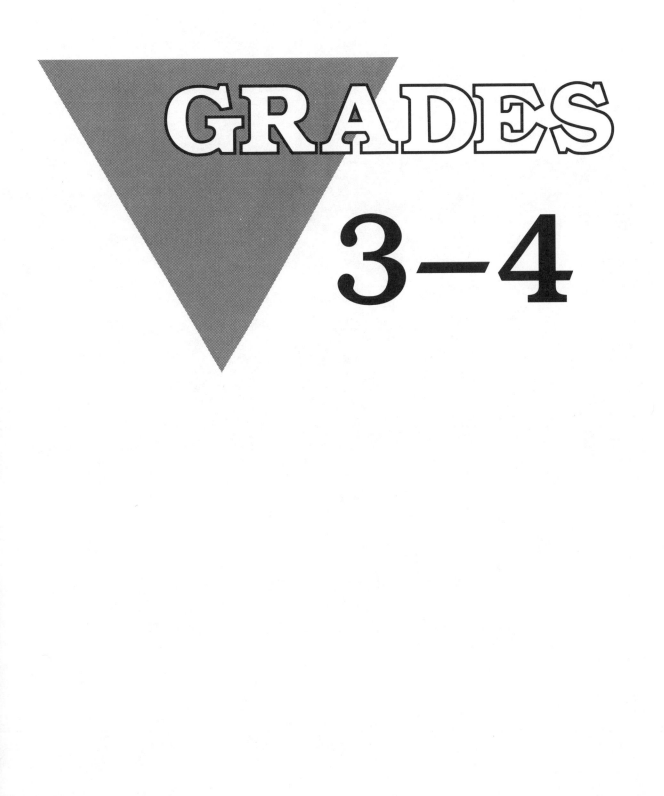

GRADES

3-4

SELF-ACCEPTANCE

Just Different

Objective

To recognize that just because people are different doesn't mean they are better or worse

Materials

Pencils as needed

Procedure

1. Introduce the activity by asking students to get out a pencil that they have been using and to bring it to the front of the room. Explain that you will be talking about differences and that they will be using their pencils to do an experiment.
2. Ask students to examine their pencils carefully, looking for special characteristics that might help them identify the pencils. Then instruct them to put their pencils into one common pile.
3. Mix the pencils up. Then, one by one, ask each student to locate his or her pencil.

Discussion

Content Questions

1. How many of you were able to find your own pencil without much difficulty? How did you do this?
2. What specific characteristics distinguished your pencil from someone else's?
3. Suppose that we had put people instead of pencils into the pile. Are there specific characteristics that distinguish people from one another?
4. Just because you or your pencil is different, does that make you or it better than another? Worse?
5. What problems might occur if everyone or everything were identical?

Personalization Questions

1. In what ways are you different from other people?
2. What do you think about these differences? Are you glad that you have them? Do you feel OK about them?

To the Leader

Stress the point that differences are good and that we don't need to compare ourselves with others and assume that they are better or worse just because such differences exist.

Nobody Likes Me

Objective

To recognize that it's not possible for everyone to like or love you

Materials

Story "Nobody Likes Me"

Procedure

1. Ask students to raise a hand if they've ever thought to themselves, "Nobody likes me." You may want to ask for examples of who they think doesn't like them, such as parents, siblings, friends, teachers, etc.

2. Invite students to listen to the story to see if they can identify with the characters. After reading the story, discuss.

Nobody Likes Me

Nicky walked in from recess and quietly sat down. She felt absolutely horrible because while she was standing in line she heard Sally and Carrie talking about being invited to Lynn's birthday party. Why wasn't she invited? She and Lynn were friends, too. "What did I do? Why doesn't she like me anymore?" These questions were rumbling around in Nicky's mind all afternoon. The teacher even had to get mad at her for not paying attention.

When Nicky got home from school, she went straight to her room. She tried to do her homework, but she was too upset to concentrate. Finally, she decided to go down to get a snack. As she wandered into the kitchen, her brother Todd asked, "Hey, what's bugging you?"

"Oh, nothing," said Nicky. "I just had a bad day."

"Come on," said Todd, "You'll feel better if you talk about it. What happened?"

So Nicky told him that she didn't get invited to Lynn's birthday party and she didn't know why because she knew that they were friends. "Look," said Todd, "Just because Lynn didn't invite you doesn't mean she doesn't like you. Maybe she doesn't, but did you ever think about the fact that maybe she can only invite a couple of kids? It doesn't have to mean that she doesn't like you."

"Well, I suppose you're right, but I still feel bad."

"It's OK to feel bad," said Todd, "but it's not OK to go around thinking that you're no good or that you did something wrong just because she didn't invite you. Besides that, I guess you just have to learn that it's not possible for everyone to like you."

Nicky thought about what Todd had told her, and, although she still wished that she had been invited, she felt better. "At least there's nothing wrong with me," she said to herself.

Discussion

Content Questions

1. Why did Nicky think that Lynn didn't like her?
2. What was the real reason that Lynn didn't invite Nicky to the party?
3. Suppose that Nicky really didn't like Lynn. Would this mean that there was something wrong with Lynn or that she wasn't a good person?

Personalization Questions

1. Have you ever been in a situation like this, in which you assumed that someone didn't like you, but in fact that wasn't true? Share examples.
2. Just because someone doesn't always pay attention to you or invite you places or show interest in what you're doing, does this mean that they don't like you? What does it mean?
3. Suppose that someone really doesn't like you. Do you think that it is possible to be liked by everyone?
4. If someone doesn't like you, are you still a good person?

To the Leader

It is very important for children to realize that they often assume that people don't like them when in fact these people may or may not. It is equally important for them to understand that, even if someone dislikes them, they're still OK.

Put-Downs

Objective

To learn about self put-downs and their effect

Materials

Paper bag decorated with a large "sad face"; on the outside of the bag, negative expressions (*pig, idiot, stupid, no good, fat slob, ugly, crazy*); inside the bag, on slips of paper, additional negative expressions (*nothing I try works, dummy, no good, goofed again, stupid, ugly, fat, the worst, dingbat, freak, ignorant, creep*)

Procedure

1. Share the paper bag with the students and have them take turns reading the words on the outside. Explain that these are put-downs, and that put-downs can be given by other people to you or you can give them to yourself. Self put-downs are the focus of the activity.
2. Ask for several volunteers to draw a slip of paper out of the bag. When these students have their slips, ask them to read the words printed on them out loud, as if talking to themselves.
3. If there are more slips, have more volunteers follow the same procedure.

Discussion

Content Questions

1. How did you feel when you gave yourself a put-down?
2. Have you ever said words like this to yourself before? Share examples.

Personalization Questions

1. What do you accomplish by putting yourself down?
2. Even if you do make some mistakes, does it help the situation to get upset with yourself?
3. How can you stop yourself from saying these things?

To the Leader

Emphasize that, even when one does make a mistake or do something unfortunate, self put-downs often make the situation worse.

So They Say

Objective

To distinguish between what people say about you and who you are

Materials

So They Say Scripts (Handout 5)

Procedure

1. Ask for a show of hands from children who have been teased at some time in their lives. Discuss the fact that, although we can't usually prevent someone from teasing us or calling us names, it is important to decide whether the tease or the name is really "who we are."

2. Invite four volunteers to enact the So They Say Script (Handout 5). Give each volunteer a copy of the script and explain the essence of each character's role to the players.

3. Discuss the Content Questions.

4. Next, without revealing who has teased them, have students brainstorm names they have been called or have heard others be called, such as *pig, dumb, four-eyes*, etc. Discuss the Personalization Questions.

Discussion

Content Questions

1. To the child being teased (Kid #1): How did you feel about the comments?

2. Do you think that there would have been any way to prevent the children on the bus from teasing about the braces?

3. What do you think about the way that the child being teased decided to cope with the situation?

Personalization Questions

1. When you have been called names in the past, what was said about you?

2. What does it really mean if people tease you? Are you what they say you are? Are you less worthwhile because of what they say?

3. What have you learned?

To the Leader

Children need to understand that, although they can't control anyone else's behavior, they can control their own reactions to people by recognizing that they aren't what others say they are.

HANDOUT 5

So They Say Script

The Scene: On the bus going to school. Kid #1 has just gotten braces.

Kid #2   Walks onto the bus, notices Kid #1's braces, and points them out to friends, Kids #3 and #4.

Kid #1:   Starts talking to the friend s/he is sitting with.

Kid #2:   Leans across the aisle, smiles widely and points to his/her mouth, making criss-cross signs on teeth.

Kid #3:   Laughs and says to Kid #1, "Hey wire-face, what are you doin'?"

Kid #1:   Just sits there and doesn't say anything.

Kid #4:   Stands up and announces in a loud voice, "Hey, everybody! There's a new brace-face on the bus. If anyone needs any metal, they know where they can get it!"

Kid #1:   Starts talking again to the friend s/he is sitting with.

Kid #2:   Says loudly to his/her friends, "Hey, s/he better not talk too much or his/her tongue will get caught up in all those wires."

Kid #1:   Getting irritated, but says to his/her friend, "It won't do any good to get mad at them. I know I'm not a 'brace-face,' so I'm not going to let what they say bother me."

I Can Try

Objective

To learn that trying or doing your best, regardless of final outcome, is important

Materials

A book from each student's desk

Procedure

1. Introduce the activity by asking a few students to share examples of a time that they tried to do something that they thought might be hard or that they didn't think they could do at all. Discuss what happened when they tried, how they felt about trying, etc.

2. Invite students to participate in some short experiments:

   Stand on only your left foot, keeping your right one in the air for 30 seconds (no props).

   Stand on only your right foot, with your left in the air for 30 seconds (no props).

   Walk around the room for 30 seconds balancing a book on your head.

Discussion

Content Questions

1. Before trying the experiments, how many of you thought that you could do them?
2. If you weren't able to do them, do you wish that you hadn't tried?
3. What do you think is good about trying to do things like this?

Personalization Questions

1. What is something that you've tried to do but haven't been able to? Share experiences.
2. If you can't do things that you try, what does it mean?
3. Do you think that it is better to try and maybe fail or not to try at all?
4. Can you share an experience that has happened to you when you haven't tried to do something and later wished you had?

To the Leader

Reinforcing the idea that trying helps, not hurts, is important. If children try and fail, their failure doesn't mean that they are not competent or will never learn the particular task.

Perfectly, Perfectly

Objective

To recognize that perfection is impossible and that not being perfect doesn't mean you're incompetent

Materials

Nine tennis balls

Procedure

1. Ask if there are any students who have ever done anything perfectly. Take three volunteers and ask each of them to juggle three tennis balls perfectly. Ask other students to be observers who will look for the task to be perfectly done. After several minutes, stop the activity.

Discussion

Content Questions

1. To the observers: Was anyone able to do this task perfectly?
2. To the volunteers: How did you feel about not doing the task perfectly?
3. Are there people in this world who can juggle perfectly? Can they do it every time they try?
4. How many think that the people who didn't juggle perfectly are stupid and unable to do things well?

Personalization Questions

1. Have you ever tried to do something perfectly but not succeeded?
2. What does it mean if you don't do all things perfectly? Does it mean you're not competent or that you don't do anything well?
3. What have you learned about doing things perfectly?

To the Leader

It is important that children recognize the impossibility of constant perfection and that they avoid equating their worth with how well they do things.

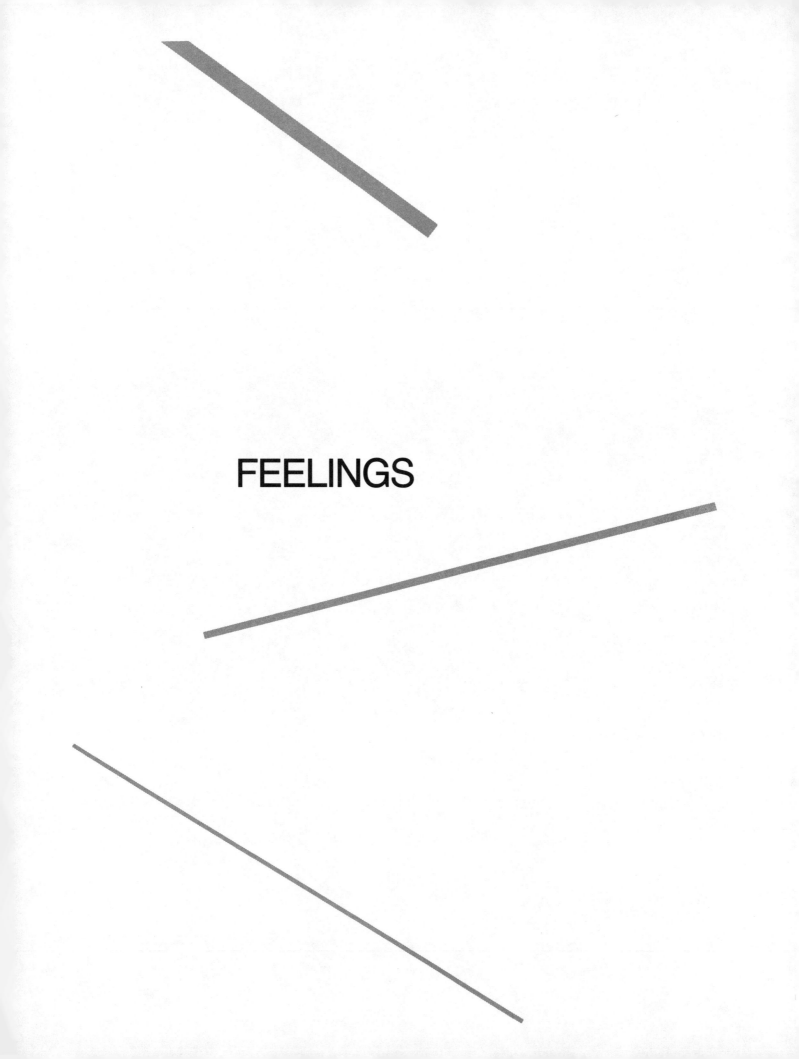

FEELINGS

Face Your Feelings

Objective

To recognize that people can feel differently about the same event

Materials

Four paper plates per student; markers or crayons as needed

Procedure

1. Ask students to draw faces on their paper plates to represent the following emotions: happy, sad, angry, and worried.

2. Explain to students that you will be reading some situations and that they are to think about how they feel when they experience a situation like the ones they are hearing.

3. Read each of the following situations one at a time, instructing students to respond by flipping up the face they think shows the appropriate feeling. Before reading another situation, ask students to check to see how others have responded. If not everyone responded in the same way, ask why students think some people feel differently about the same situation. (For example, some people might feel happy about snow because they like to ski, whereas others might be angry because it will prevent them from going out of town.) Continue with the other situations, again discussing responses.

   It is going to snow tonight.

   Your cousins are coming to visit.

   Your parents are taking you shopping after school.

   Your teacher is keeping you in for recess.

   You didn't get picked for the volleyball team.

   You might move to a different town.

   You are going into a new reading group.

   Your dad or mom just got a new job.

   Your friend is moving.

   You've been sick and can't participate in physical education.

Discussion

Content Questions

1. Did everyone respond to a given situation with the same feeling? If not, why do you think this happened?

2. Do you think that there is any situation in which all people would feel exactly the same?

3. Why do you think two people can feel differently about the same situation?

Personalization Questions

1. Do you think it is all right to feel differently from someone else about something? Has this ever happened to you? Share examples.

2. What did you learn from this activity?

To the Leader

This activity focuses on the fact that feelings are really very individual; in addition, it introduces the concept that people's feelings differ because they have different thoughts.

I Think, I Feel

Objective

To learn that feelings come from thoughts

Materials

Paper and pencils as needed

Procedure

1. Read the following situations, stopping at the points marked *feeling* and asking each student to write down a word describing how he or she would feel in that situation.

> You are riding your bike down the street when a kid yells, "Hey, you, don't steal my bike! Bring my bike back!"
>
> Feeling _____
>
> Then, when you stop and are ready to tell the kid that it is your own bike, the kid looks closer and says, "Oh, I'm sorry. I thought it was mine. I just got it with money I'd been saving for two years."
>
> Feeling _____
>
> You're in a store and a grown woman nearly knocks you over as she runs out the door.
>
> Feeling _____
>
> In a couple of minutes you hear someone say that her child has just been taken by ambulance to the hospital.
>
> Feeling _____
>
> You are walking down the hall to your class and accidentally bump into a fifth-grade girl. She turns around and really yells at you, telling you what a clumsy jerk you are.
>
> Feeling _____
>
> Later that day, she apologizes to you, saying that she was in a bad mood because she had studied for a social studies test and still got a bad grade.
>
> Feeling _____

2. Share the feeling words identified for each of the situations.

Discussion

Content Questions

1. Did your feelings change in each of the situations? Why do you think they changed?

2. Did everyone feel the same way about these situations? Why do you suppose some people had different feelings?

3. How do you think feelings change?

Personalization Questions

1. Can you think of any situations you've experienced in which your feelings changed once you learned more about the situation? Share examples.

2. What do you think you can do to change your feelings about a situation?

To the Leader

This activity will illustrate that, when thoughts change or new information is shared, feelings may also change. It is important to emphasize that students can change how they feel about an event by changing what they think about it.

How Strong?

Objective

To learn that feelings vary in intensity

Materials

Three cans (one labeled *Strong*, one *Mild*, and one *Weak)*; How Strong Situations Lists (Handout 6); scissors as needed

Procedure

1. Introduce the activity by discussing how feelings vary in intensity. (For example, sometimes we are very angry about something, and other times we might be mildly angry or not at all angry.) Share some examples that illustrate differences in intensity.

2. Distribute the How Strong Situations List (Handout 6) and ask students to read each situation, fill in the feelings they think they would have, and check the level of intensity of the feeling.

3. Once students have completed the feeling and intensity identification, ask them to cut the sheet of situations into individual strips.

4. Read the first situation and ask for five volunteers to state their feelings about it. Have them then place their strips in the cans corresponding to the intensity levels they identified. Make sure that all students see the cans into which the strips go. Do the same, with different volunteers, for several more situations.

Discussion

Content Questions

1. Did you all respond to a given situation with the same feeling?
2. Did you all respond to a given situation with the same intensity?
3. What do you think accounts for the differences in feelings or intensity of feelings?

Personalization Questions

1. Have you ever been in a situation in which you felt very strongly about something and then later didn't feel so strongly? Share examples.
2. Have you ever changed the intensity of your feelings? How did you do that?

To the Leader

Helping students recognize that feelings vary in intensity creates the awareness that people don't always have to feel strongly about certain events and that, in time, intensity diminishes. Reinforce the idea that feelings can be more easily managed when thoughts change.

HANDOUT 6

How Strong Situations List

Directions: Read each of the situations. Identify how you might feel in the situation and how strongly you would feel about the event.

1. Someone steals your bike.

   Feeling _____ Strong _____ Mild _____ Weak _____

2. Your parents ground you for the week.

   Feeling _____ Strong _____ Mild _____ Weak _____

3. Your best friend moves away.

   Feeling _____ Strong _____ Mild _____ Weak _____

4. You have a test tomorrow in math.

   Feeling _____ Strong _____ Mild _____ Weak _____

5. You are going shopping for new clothes.

   Feeling _____ Strong _____ Mild _____ Weak _____

6. You have been elected class president.

   Feeling _____ Strong _____ Mild _____ Weak _____

7. Someone calls you a stupid jerk.

   Feeling _____ Strong _____ Mild _____ Weak _____

8. You have just won first prize in a contest.

   Feeling _____ Strong _____ Mild _____ Weak _____

9. You can stay up late to watch a favorite TV show.

   Feeling _____ Strong _____ Mild _____ Weak _____

10. You can't find your coat, and the bus is coming.

    Feeling _____ Strong _____ Mild _____ Weak _____

Thermometer of Emotions

Objective

To learn that feelings can change

Materials

Thermometer of Emotions Situations; one Thermometer of Emotion per situation; pens or pencils as needed

Procedure

1. Ask students to think about a time when they have really felt scared, such as just before a big test or a recital. As they share examples, ask how they felt after that event was over. Emphasize the fact that feelings do change, sometimes because the situation changes and sometimes because our thoughts about the event change.
2. Divide students into groups of four. Give each group an equal number of situation cards and a separate Thermometer of Emotions for each situation they receive.
3. Instruct the groups to discuss their feelings about the situations and come to a consensus about the feeling they would have in response to each. On the situation cards, groups write down the feeling and indicate its intensity on a scale of 1–10. They then move the indicator on the thermometer to the appropriate "temperature."
4. Invite groups to share their situations and discuss the feelings and levels of intensity they picked for each situation.
5. Display the Thermometers of Emotion along with the corresponding situation cards on the bulletin board.

Discussion

Content Questions

1. Was it difficult to agree on the feeling and level of intensity for various situations? Were some situations more difficult than others?
2. Why do you think that some of these situations resulted in intense emotions and others didn't?
3. Why do you think that some of you felt more or less strongly about some of the situations than others did?
4. Imagine that two days have passed since the various situations occurred. Do you think your feelings would change? What do you think would happen if it were two months or two years later? Would your feelings change again? Why?

Personalization Questions

1. Can you think of a time when your feelings about something or someone changed? Why do you think this happened? Share examples.
2. Do you think feelings change just because of time, or do you think that you can do something to change your feelings? What have you done to change your feelings about something?

To the Leader

Children need to understand that feelings will change because of time, because they grow up and find different things meaningful, and because they change their thoughts or develop other coping strategies.

Thermometer of Emotions

Directions: Make the thermometers out of tagboard, with horizontal slits cut as shown. Insert a red strip of paper into the bottom slit; the top of this strip can then be pushed through an upper slit to show the intensity of the feeling. (In the example shown, the group felt moderately disappointed about losing their kickball game.)

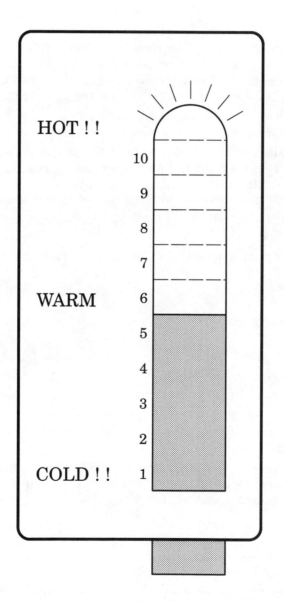

Thermometer of Emotions Situations

Directions: Copy each situation on a separate index card.

1. I didn't get to go skating.
   Emotion _____ Rating _____

2. Andy didn't ask me to stay over.
   Emotion _____ Rating _____

3. Someone told me I was stupid.
   Emotion _____ Rating _____

4. I didn't win the checkers game.
   Emotion _____ Rating _____

5. I got accused of cheating.
   Emotion _____ Rating _____

6. Someone made fun of my new shirt.
   Emotion _____ Rating _____

7. I got a *F* on a test.
   Emotion _____ Rating _____

8. I got sent to the office.
   Emotion _____ Rating _____

9. I missed the bus.
   Emotion _____ Rating _____

10. Kids on the bus teased me.
    Emotion _____ Rating _____

11. I got teased about my weight.
    Emotion _____ Rating _____

12. My mom went to the hospital.
    Emotion _____ Rating _____

13. My grandma died.
    Emotion _____ Rating _____

14. My team lost the kickball game.
    Emotion _____ Rating _____

15. I didn't get invited to a party.
    Emotion _____ Rating _____

16. I didn't know how to do my math.
    Emotion _____ Rating _____

17. I lost some money.
    Emotion _____ Rating _____

18. My parents yelled at me.
    Emotion _____ Rating _____

19. My dog is sick.
    Emotion _____ Rating _____

20. I won a contest.
    Emotion _____ Rating _____

I Feel, I Do

Objective

To learn to differentiate between a feeling and a behavior

Materials

I Feel, I Do Worksheets (Handout 7); pens or pencils as needed; a large envelope; individual strips of paper, on which are written the following feeling words: *awful, helpless, terrible, gloomy, hateful, confused, scared, angry, hurt, embarrassed, jealous, ashamed, mixed up, guilty, discouraged, frustrated, worried, sad, excited, happy*

Procedure

1. Place the strips of paper on which the words are written in the large envelope. Divide students into groups of four and have each child in each group draw a feeling word out of the envelope. (If there are more than 20 students, generate more words.)

2. Explain that each of the strips of paper contains a feeling word, and that, usually, when we experience a feeling, we behave in certain ways. (For example, if you are angry, you might throw something, call someone a name, or mumble to yourself.)

3. After making sure that students see the distinction between feelings and behaviors, distribute one I Feel, I Do Worksheet (Handout 7) per group. Ask each group member to read his or her feeling word aloud and write it on the worksheet under the heading *Feelings*. Then have students brainstorm as a group all of the ways that they have behaved when they have had that feeling. They are to list these on the sheet under the heading *Behaviors*.

4. When groups have completed the task, ask students to share examples of feelings and behaviors.

Discussion

Content Questions

1. Could you identify behaviors for all the feelings?
2. Do you typically have more behaviors for positive or negative feelings?
3. Why do you think it is important to understand about feelings and behaviors?

Personalization Questions

1. Do you think that, just because you have a certain feeling, you have to behave in a certain way? Is there an example of a time when you have felt a particular way and have chosen to act one way instead of another? Share.

2. Are there behaviors that you would like to change and not have to experience when you have a particular feeling? Share examples.

To the Leader

Helping children see that they have a choice about behavior when experiencing feelings gives them more control over their lives.

I Feel, I Do Worksheet

Directions: List your feeling words on the paper under the heading *Feelings*. Then, under the heading *Behaviors*, write down several ways that you behave when you feel this way.

Feelings   **Behaviors**

1. _____   _____

                                                          _____

                                                          _____

2. _____   _____

                                                          _____

                                                          _____

3. _____   _____

                                                          _____

                                                          _____

4. _____   _____

                                                          _____

                                                          _____

How Do You Feel?

Objective

To learn that there are many different ways of expressing feelings

Materials

How Do You Feel Situations List

Procedure

1. Divide the class into teams of three and designate a leader for each group. Give each team a situation card from the How Do You Feel Situations List.
2. Instruct each leader to read the situation to his or her team members. As a team, they are to identify one word to describe how they might feel in that situation.
3. Ask Team 1's leader to read their situation aloud to the class and identify the feeling word they selected. Each member of that team simultaneously acts out how he or she would express that feeling. The rest of the class looks for similarities and differences in expressing the feeling.
4. Stop and discuss the Content Questions.
5. Continue this procedure with the remaining teams, then discuss the Personalization Questions.

Discussion

Content Questions

1. Did everyone in the team express the same feeling in the same way? What were the similarities or differences?
2. Do you think there is just one way to express a feeling?
3. Do you think you have to express your feelings in the same way someone else does? Why is or isn't expressing yourself in the same way as someone else a good idea?

Personalization Questions

1. When you have certain feelings, is it hard for you to express them? Which feelings are more difficult to express than others?
2. Have you had an experience in which you and someone else expressed a feeling about the same situation in a different way? Share examples.

To the Leader

Enough situations for eight groups are provided; more can be generated if necessary.

How Do You Feel Situations List

Directions: Copy each situation on a separate index card.

1. You are being blamed for something you didn't do.

2. A classmate pushes you at the drinking fountain.

3. You earn an award for being the most responsible student in your class.

4. Your family won a free trip to Disneyworld.

5. Your sister tells your parents that you were watching TV when you were supposed to be studying.

6. Someone stole your new school backpack.

7. When you were dressing after physical education class, you couldn't find your underwear.

8. You ate five cookies after school when you were only supposed to have one.

BELIEFS AND BEHAVIOR

Facts and Beliefs

Objective

To differentiate between facts and beliefs

Materials

Facts and Beliefs Game Boards (Handout 8); pens or pencils as needed

Procedure

1. Introduce the activity by asking students what a fact is (something that can be proven to be true, such as the statement "The sun is shining today") and what a belief is (an opinion or your idea about something, such as the statement "The sunshine is too hot").

2. Divide students into pairs and nominate one partner in each pair to be in charge of facts, the other beliefs. Distribute one Facts and Beliefs Game Board (Handout 8) to each pair, explaining that they will play a game like Tic-Tac-Toe. When a statement is read by the leader, the class discusses whether it is a fact or a belief. If it is determined to be a fact, the partner in charge of facts puts an *F* on the game board. If it is a belief, the partner in charge of beliefs puts a *B* on the board. The first person to get three *F*'s or three *B*'s in a row is the winner.

3. Read the statements below, continuing the game until someone has three *F*'s or three *B*'s in a row.

> Corn is a vegetable. (fact)
>
> Kids who go to this school are wonderful. (belief)
>
> Snowmobiling is great! (belief)
>
> All golden retrievers are very smart dogs. (belief)
>
> Kickball is a game. (fact)
>
> Summer is the best season of the year. (belief)
>
> Milk comes from cows. (fact)
>
> Basketball is a sport. (fact)
>
> Girls are smarter than boys. (belief)

Discussion

Content Questions

1. Was it difficult to figure out which statements were facts and which were beliefs? What helps you to understand the difference?

2. Do all people have the same beliefs about a given fact? For example, do all people think the same thing about the fact that the Iowa Hawkeyes (or your own state team) have basketball and football teams? Some people may believe that the teams are good and some may believe that the teams are not good. (Invite students to share examples of beliefs about different facts.)

Personalization Questions

1. Can you think of a fact about yourself? What about a belief about that fact? (For example, someone might play basketball, and the belief might be that he or she plays it well.)

To the Leader

It is important to help students see that facts can be proven and that it is often the beliefs about the facts that create problems among people.

HANDOUT 8

Facts and Beliefs Game Board

Directions: Play this game like Tic-Tac-Toe. When you hear a fact, the partner in charge of facts should put an *F* on the board. When you hear a belief, the partner in charge of beliefs should put a *B* on the board. The first person with three *F*'s or three *B*'s in a row wins.

Beliefs, Feelings, and Behaviors

Objective

To recognize the connection between feelings, beliefs, and behaviors

Materials

Masking tape

Procedure

1. With masking tape, make a long line on the floor. Identify one end as being extremely positive and the other as being extremely negative. Tell students that you will be reading some statements to them and that you will be asking volunteers to "take a stand" on the line in a place demonstrating their reaction to the statement.

2. Ask for five volunteers and have them take a position on the line relative to the following statements. Ask other students to be observers.

    You'll have a new teacher starting next week.

    You're having spaghetti for lunch.

    You're moving to a new town.

3. Stop and discuss the first two Content Questions.

4. Ask for five more volunteers and ask them to take a position on the following statements.

    You have to stay in for recess.

    Your parents are going out, and you'll have a sitter.

    Your grandma bought you a new shirt.

5. Stop and discuss the last two Content Questions and the Personalization Questions.

Discussion

Content Questions

1. Did everyone stand on the line in exactly the same place?

2. The situation was the same for all volunteers, but they responded differently. What caused this to happen? (Discuss the fact that people think differently about situations. Elicit some various thoughts about one or two of the situations.)

3. Different people had different beliefs or ideas about each situation. How did this fact affect their feelings (positive or negative) about the situation?

4. Do you think that people's beliefs and feelings about situations would also affect their behavior? Explain.

Personalization Questions

1. Can you think of a time when your beliefs about a situation affected your feelings about it? Did your beliefs also affect your behavior? Invite students to share examples.

To the Leader

Stress that children have positive or negative feelings because of the beliefs they have about the situations in which they find themselves.

Checking It Out

Objective

To develop the skill of checking out the facts

Materials

None

Procedure

1. Review the definition of a fact (something that can be proven true or untrue).
2. Write the name of each student on the chalkboard. Then ask students to think of a personal fact about themselves and record these facts on the board next to their names.
3. Ask for a volunteer to be "It." Instruct that person to close his or her eyes and point to one of the names on the board. "It" then writes down an assumption (something believed to be true) about the person whose name he or she picked. For example, the fact about John might be that he has blue eyes; the assumption might be that he likes to play hockey. The person whose name was picked then verifies whether or not the assumption was true. If so, "It" puts an *F* beside it; if not, he or she puts an *A*.
4. Select another person to be "It" and follow the same procedure. Repeat several times so that students have a chance to make and check out assumptions.

Discussion

Content Questions

1. Can assumptions be facts? How can you find out?
2. What might happen if you assumed that something was a fact and didn't check it out?
3. What is the difference between a fact and an assumption?

Personalization Questions

1. Have you ever made an assumption about someone or something and didn't check it out? What happened?
2. Has someone ever made an assumption about you and not checked it out? Did anything happen as a result of this?
3. Why is it important to check out assumptions?

To the Leader

If children don't check out assumptions, they may act on erroneous information. It is possible for one assumption to cause a chain reaction of negativity in relationships.

Stop, Go, and Caution

Objective

To learn to recognize the negative consequences of acting on assumptions

Materials

Story "Stop, Go, and Caution"

Procedure

1. Explain what it means to be cautious. Read the story, then discuss.

Stop, Go, and Caution

It was Monday morning. Debbie had been up late on both Friday and Saturday nights, and last night her parents were arguing so she couldn't get to sleep. She was really afraid that they were going to get a divorce because they had been yelling a lot lately. As she got on the bus, all she could think about was which parent she would live with if they did get a divorce and whether or not she would have to change schools. When Dana got on the bus, Debbie was lost in her own thoughts and just mumbled hello. Dana sat across the aisle and wondered why Debbie was being so rude to her.

The bus arrived at school, and it turned out Debbie was Dana's math partner. Debbie hardly said a word and didn't help much with the work. Dana felt angry because she resented doing all the work. After math, they had recess. Dana deliberately ignored Debbie and, in fact, teased her about being so quiet. During recess, all Debbie could think about was the fact that her parents were probably talking about the divorce. She wondered if it had anything to do with her. She had been sort of bad lately, fighting a lot with her sister.

On the bus ride home after school, Debbie once again was very quiet. Finally, Dana asked her why she had been so lazy during math time and why Debbie didn't like her anymore. Debbie explained that she was worried about her parents, so Dana realized that she had been wrong to assume that it was something she had done and apologized for being cruel at recess.

When Debbie got home, she decided to ask her parents about the divorce, just as Dana had asked her what was wrong. Her mother explained that all parents fight once in a while but that doesn't mean that they are getting a divorce. Debbie was relieved and wished she'd asked earlier so that she could have enjoyed her day!

Discussion

Content Questions

1. What happened when Debbie acted on her assumption? What happened when Dana acted on hers?
2. What happened when Debbie and Dana checked out their assumptions?

1. Have you ever acted like the people in this story? What happened in your situation?
2. Has acting on your assumptions ever resulted in positive experiences? If not, what can you do to avoid having negative consequences result when you make assumptions?

To the Leader

Stress the importance of checking out before acting on assumptions. Frequently, children get carried away with their assumptions; this tendency often results in unnecessary worries, inappropriate reactionary behavior, and other problems.

Options

Objective

To learn behavioral alternatives for expressing negative emotions

Materials

Options Situations Lists (Handout 9)

Procedure

1. Discuss the fact that, even though people have negative feelings, they do have choices about how to express those feelings through their actions.

2. Divide students into pairs. Distribute one Options Situations List (Handout 9) per pair and have students work together to develop a response to each situation. Discuss.

Discussion

Content Questions

1. Was it difficult to think of alternative ways of behaving? Were any of the situations more difficult than others?

2. Just because someone may feel a certain way about a situation, what does that mean in terms of their behavior?

Personalization Questions

1. When you have negative emotions, do you consider different ways to behave? What influences your thinking about how to behave?

2. Do you think you have to feel a certain way and then act a certain way, or can you change how you feel and act?

To the Leader

Children need to realize that, even though they have negative feelings, they can choose how to behave. Recognizing options is important. After receiving guidance, children can more independently assume this behavior.

HANDOUT 9

Options Situations List

Directions: Read each situation and decide whether or not you would select option a or b. If you can think of another option, write it down in the space marked c.

1. Your parents won't get you the "in look" jacket that you want because it costs too much. You are disappointed. You:

   a. Save your own money to buy one.

   b. Say to your parents, "You're selfish. You never get me what I want."

   c. _____

2. You want to go bowling, but your parent says you can't go. You are upset. You:

   a. Go to your room and find something else to do.

   b. Slam the door and throw a book across the room.

   c. _____

3. You get a bad grade on a test. You:

   a. Cry about it.

   b. Study harder the next time.

   c. _____

4. Your team loses a game. You:

   a. Shrug it off.

   b. Blame the umpire.

   c. _____

5. You make several mistakes at a music recital. You:

   a. Just say to yourself that you tried to do well.

   b. Slam your piano book on the keyboard.

   c. _____

It's Awful!

Objective

To identify examples of "awfulized thinking" and to recognize that our beliefs contribute to this type of thinking.

Materials

It's Awful! Situations; paper bag; pens or pencils as needed

Procedure

1. Clip the It's Awful! Situations so that all of the 1's, 2's, etc. are together. Place them in a paper bag decorated with a "doom and gloom" face on the front.

2. Introduce the activity by showing students the paper bag and indicating that the reason the person depicted on the bag looks so gloomy is that he or she has had several rotten days . . . everything has gone wrong, and everything is absolutely awful. Ask students to define what the word *awful* means and to give some examples of what they think is awful. List these on the chalkboard.

3. Explain that inside the bag are situations some people may consider awful. Ask for five volunteers who are going to be the "awfulizer raters." Their job is to rate these situations as to their degree of awfulness. (The scale goes from 1–5, with 1 being very, very awful and 5 being not awful at all.)

4. Ask one volunteer to draw a set of situations from the bag and distribute the strips to each of the other volunteers. As the situation is read by the volunteer, each of the other volunteers writes a rating number on his or her own situation slip. Tape the slips to the outside of the bag as the ratings are shared.

5. Distribute another set of situations to a new set of volunteers and follow the same procedure.

Discussion

Content Questions

1. Did everyone rate the situations the same way?

2. Why do you think some people rated the situations as being more awful than others did? (You may want to reread some of the situations and compare the differences in ratings.)

3. Since some people don't feel awful about the same things you do, it must mean that what you think about the situation makes a difference. If you change your thinking about what you thought was awful, what do you suppose might happen?

4. Just because something seems awful now, does that mean it will always seem awful?

1. Share an example of something that seemed awful to you but might not have been for someone else. What made it awful for you? Was it really awful, or not so awful when compared to other things?

2. Next time you think something is awful, what can you do to feel better?

To the Leader

Children need to be able to put awfulizing in perspective and realize that what we think about events determines the extent to which something seems really awful. Some of the ways children can make themselves feel better are talking to someone, remembering that "awful" doesn't last forever, or doing a pleasant activity.

It's Awful! Situations

Directions: Copy each situation on five separate slips of paper, then clip together.

1. A tornado destroyed your house.
2. You didn't get invited to a skating party.
3. Your grandpa died.
4. You got a haircut that looks ugly.
5. You got a bad grade on a paper.
6. Your dad lost his job.
7. You didn't get what you wanted for your birthday.
8. Your cat is sick.

PROBLEM SOLVING/
DECISION MAKING

What Happens When . . .

Objective

To recognize the cause-effect relationship in the decision-making process

Materials

None

Procedure

1. Review the nature of the cause-effect relationship as developed in Problem-Solving/ Decision-Making Activity 1 for Grades 1–2 (Decisions and Consequences).
2. Ask for volunteers to role play each of the following interactions.

    Two participants: Two friends are having lunch together at school. One friend shares half of a special treat with the other, and they both feel good.

    Several participants: A group of children are playing together on the playground. One child accuses another of cheating during the course of the game, and a fight breaks out.

    Two participants: A child is studying for a spelling test. A friend calls to suggest they go out to play instead. The next day, the child misses two words on the test.

3. Direct an analysis of cause-effect demonstrated in each of the role-play situations.
4. Assign the students to small groups (4–6 participants) and have them prepare an original dramatization of a cause-effect situation. Discuss each with the class following its presentation.

Discussion

Content Questions

1. How are behaviors (causes) related to consequences (effects)?
2. What control do we have over the things that happen to us?

Personalization Questions

1. Have you ever caused a good thing to happen by a choice you made? A bad thing?
2. What things in your life would you like to change? What can you do to make a change for the better?

To the Leader

This activity extends the content of the Decisions and Consequences lesson. If students have not already participated in this earlier activity, it should be revised for grade-level appropriateness and substituted for the present lesson.

Once Upon a Time

Objective

To develop the ability to generate alternative solutions to problems

Materials

Magazine pictures, tagboard, yarn, fabric remnants, tongue depressors, glue, scissors, and crayons as needed

Procedure

1. Display magazine pictures of people in some sort of problem-solving or decision-making situation, such as a person with a household crisis, a shopper choosing between two different products, or a child in an argument with a friend. Discuss and list different things each person pictured might do. Encourage multiple responses.
2. Explain that, normally, more than one solution exists to any problem or decision we face. Stress the importance of taking time to consider alternatives before acting.
3. Discuss the decisions made by main characters in each of the following familiar stories: *The Three Bears* (Goldilocks' decision to enter the house), *Jack and the Beanstalk* (Jack's decision to sell the cow), *Hansel and Gretel* (the children's decision to run away). Allow students to suggest other familiar stories and explore each for examples of decision-making behavior.
4. Invite groups of students to construct stick puppets and dramatize one of these three stories, changing the events and outcomes by having the main character select an alternative solution to the problem.
5. Have each group present to the class the decision-making behavior and alternatives selected.

Discussion

Content Questions

1. Is there usually only one solution to a problem?
2. Why is it best to consider as many alternatives as possible before making a decision?
3. What can you do if one choice you make does not solve your problem satisfactorily?

Personalization Questions

1. Have you ever failed to solve a problem you had? What things could you have tried that you did not?
2. If you cannot think of alternatives for a decision you're trying to make or a problem you have now, what can you do to help yourself? Who are some people you know who might be helpful to talk to?

To the Leader

A major problem many children encounter in considering alternatives is their basically impulsive nature. Stress taking time to consider alternatives. Even encouraging students to try such simple strategies as counting to 10 or talking things over with a friend before taking action can help. Reminding students of this aspect of effective decision-making in daily classroom life will help reinforce the concept.

For Better or Worse

Objective

To learn to evaluate the effectiveness of possible solutions

Materials

Pictures of *Peanuts* cartoon characters (Charlie Brown, Lucy, Snoopy); For Better or Worse Think Sheets (Handout 10)

Procedure

1. Review the concept of considering alternatives in the decision-making process.

2. Show the pictures of the *Peanuts* characters as you tell each of the corresponding brief stories. Invite students to share solutions to each problem before reading the next character's problem.

> Charlie Brown: The kids have been teasing Charlie Brown about not being good at baseball. He has a chance to take practice lessons in baseball after school, or he could quit the team. He wants the kids to stop teasing him. What would be best to do? Why?

> Lucy: Lucy has to babysit her little brother, Linus, after school. She wants to go to a friend's party. She has the choice of taking her brother along, leaving him home alone, or asking her mom to have the neighbor babysit him. What would be best? Why?

> Snoopy: A new little boy in the neighborhood sees Snoopy at the playground and thinks he is a stray. The boy wants to take Snoopy home. He promises Snoopy a special dinner if he will follow the boy home. Snoopy can go with the boy and get his dinner and then run away later or go straight home to Charlie Brown. What would be best? Why?

3. Summarize the students' own conclusions from the discussion, making sure they understand that some alternatives are better than others. Direct them to use their imaginations and powers of prediction in thinking about alternatives.

4. Assign each student a Think Sheet (Handout 10) to complete. Allow time after students complete the sheets for small-group sharing of answers.

Discussion

Content Questions

1. Of the various alternatives shared in the groups, which ones seemed best to you?

2. What do you think makes one alternative better than another?

3. What can you do if you're not sure whether an alternative is good or not?

Personalization Questions

1. Have you ever had to choose between two things to do? How did you do it?

2. Have you ever made a better choice than someone else making the same kind of choice? What made your choice better?

To the Leader

Once again, this concept can be most effectively reinforced in the context of daily classroom experiences.

HANDOUT 10

For Better or Worse Think Sheet

You are allowed to invite five friends to your birthday party. You have decided on four. You have to choose between a new girl or boy who has been very nice to you and whom you like and another girl or boy who is very popular with the other kids but who has not always been friendly towards you. What would you do? Why?

_____

_____

_____

_____

You need to get a good grade on a certain math test. You forget the answer to number 7 on the test. Your teacher leaves the room while you're taking the test. Your best friend sits right next to you and always knows all the answers in math. What would you do? Why?

_____

_____

_____

_____

The Ripple Effect

Objective

To recognize the effects of decisions on self and others

Materials

Pictures of ripples in water, storms, waves; Ripple Effect Activity Sheet (Handout 11); pens or pencils as needed

Procedure

1. Display pictures of ripples in water, storms, and waves. Direct a discussion of the far-reaching effect of a change in water level or movement (tidal waves, floods, etc.).

2. Relate human behavior to the phenomenon of ripples in water by explaining that what one person does can have a far-reaching effect on other people and on future events.

3. Draw concentric circles on the chalkboard to represent ripples in water. Label the circles as shown. Discuss the possible effect of the initial behavior "You get angry and shout at your mom" on your mom and on the rest of the family, as shown.

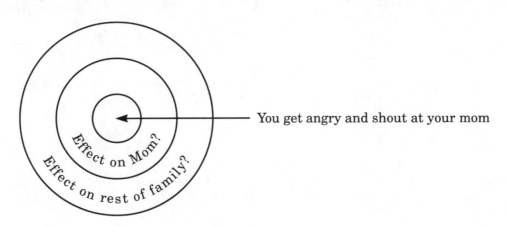

You get angry and shout at your mom

4. Develop other, similar examples, using the ripple diagram. More concentric circles can be added to show an even further extension of the possible effects of one person's behavior.

5. Assign the Activity Sheet (Handout 11); when complete, have students share in small groups (4–6 students).

Discussion

Content Questions

1. How is human behavior like a ripple in water?
2. How can we control/change the ripples we send out?
3. Can we do something to change the ripples other people send out?

Personalization Questions

1. Have you ever changed someone's day for the better by something you did? For the worse? Share experiences.

2. What ripples would you like to change at school? At home? How can you do this?

To the Leader

It is necessary to follow up this lesson by having the children illustrate and discuss examples of the ripple effect from their personal experiences. A good follow-up activity would be to have students complete and share more ripple diagrams, using examples of events occurring at home.

Ripple Effect Activity Sheet

Directions: Think about some of your actions recently that have had some kind of effect (positive or negative) on someone else. Label the ripples below for the examples you choose. Be ready to share one example with your group.

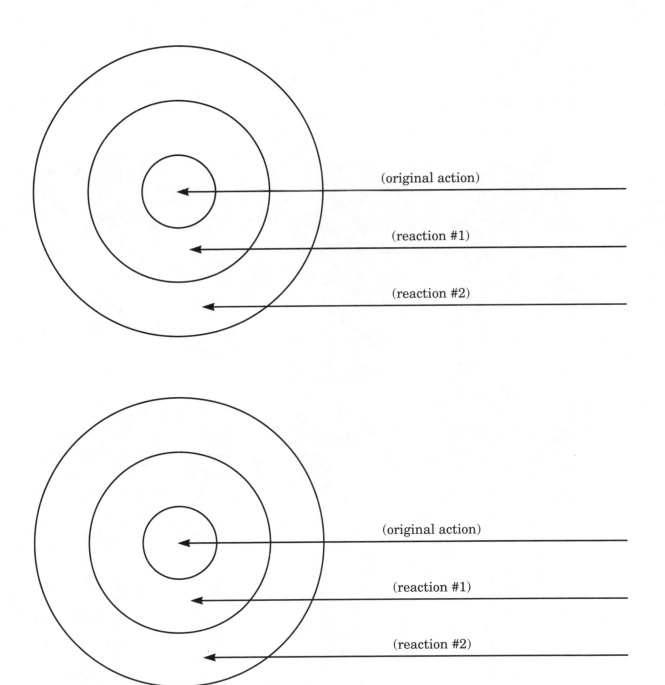

(original action)

(reaction #1)

(reaction #2)

(original action)

(reaction #1)

(reaction #2)

React and Respond

Objective

To learn to distinguish between accepting responsibility for the effects of one's decisions and blaming others

Materials

One dictionary and one 6″ × 18″ strip of manila or construction paper per student; paper and pencils as needed

Procedure

1. Write the words *reaction* and *response* on the chalkboard and have students look up and copy the definition of each.

2. Direct a discussion comparing and contrasting what it means to react versus respond.

3. Label two columns on an overhead transparency or chart paper *Reaction* and *Response*. Read the following sample behaviors and have students classify them as being either reactions or responses.

   You are suddenly frightened, and you scream.

   You are called a name, and you call a name back.

   You are being tickled, and you laugh.

   You see somebody needing help, and you help him or her.

4. Ask students to generate other examples; list these in the appropriate columns.

5. Demonstrate the meaning of the word *responsibility* by writing the word on the chalkboard and printing *response* and *ability* under corresponding components of the word. Explain that responsibility means acknowledging one's own power to choose how to act. Contrast a responsible attitude with one of blaming others by giving the following examples.

   You fail a math test and admit it's because you did not study.

   You fail a math test and tell your parents it's because the test was not fair.

6. Provide each student with a 6″ × 18″ strip of manila or construction paper. Have students fold the paper into four squares, as shown below.

1	2	3	4

7. Have students illustrate the following scene in square 1: A friend approaches you at lunch time and accuses you of tattling on him or her to the teacher that morning. In square 2, have the students illustrate a reaction they could make. In squares 3 and 4, have them illustrate two responses they might make instead that demonstrate taking control of the situation and acting in a thoughtful way to try to bring about a positive resolution.

8. Share illustrations upon completion and reinforce the idea that responsible behavior means thinking and taking control.

Discussion

Content Questions

1. What does it mean to be responsible?
2. What is the difference between taking responsibility for what happens and blaming?
3. What are the advantages of taking responsibility?
4. Why is it sometimes difficult to take responsibility for what you do?

Personalization Questions

1. Have you ever blamed someone else for what you did? How did you feel inside?
2. Have you ever taken responsibility for something you did? How did you feel inside?
3. What things in your life do you like to take responsibility for? Do you not like to take responsibility for? Why?

To the Leader

Being in the basically powerless position they are in our society, children often lack a sense of their own power and thus fail to perceive their own responsibility in effecting changes in their interactions with others. Before you can expect children to develop their sense of responsibility, you will have to encourage a sense of their inner power. A child's sense of inner power will depend in large part on his or her life experiences and self-concept and will have to be assessed individually.

R and R

Objective

To learn relaxation techniques for problem management

Materials

One throw rug or blanket per child; Relaxation Script

Procedure

1. Discuss the importance of relaxation for effective problem management. Explain that it is difficult to make good decisions when one is upset or worried and that ideas come much more easily when one is feeling relaxed.

2. Direct a progressive relaxation exercise by having the students sit or lie in a comfortable position and listen while you read the following script.

Relaxation Script

Directions: Read the script in a calm, gentle, unhurried voice, pausing between each line. Upon completion, allow students to continue discussion at their own pace. Do not rush this activity, or its benefits will be lost.

1. Concentrate on your breath.
2. Listen to the sound of your breath.
3. Coming in . . . going out . . . over . . . and over.
4. Slow your breathing down a little and listen some more.
5. Make your breaths deeper and deeper, and listen.
6. Now imagine you are living on a quiet beach.
7. It's warm.
8. No one else is around.
9. You can hear the waves.
10. They roll in to the shore . . . and out . . . in and out.
11. You can hear a bird chirping.
12. And the waves.
13. You feel warm and peaceful.
14. Feel your legs on the warm sand.
15. Tense your feet and toes up and then relax them in the sand.
16. Tense your feet up and keep them tense till I count to 10 (begin counting).
17. Now relax them and keep relaxing them till I count to 10 (begin counting).
18. Listen to the sounds of the waves.
19. Feel the warm breeze.

20. Relax your feet and toes.

21. Now tense up your leg muscles and then relax.

22. (Continue tensing and relaxing to the count of 10 for legs, body, arms, and hands. In between each muscle group, have students listen to the waves, birds, their own breath.)

Discussion

Content Questions

1. How did you feel before the relaxation exercise? During? After?

2. What does it mean to relax?

3. What are some ways you can relax?

4. How do you think relaxation can help you solve problems more creatively and effectively?

Personalization Questions

1. Can you think of a time you were very tense, nervous, or worried? Did you feel able to solve whatever your problems were when you felt like that? Share examples.

2. Can you think of some things that have helped you relax? Share.

To the Leader

There are many relaxation tapes available through local libraries; these can provide a model to follow in this directed activity.

INTERPERSONAL
RELATIONSHIPS

Judgment Machine

Objective

To learn to differentiate between judgmental and nonjudgmental attitudes toward others

Materials

A large cardboard box (decorated to be the Judgment Machine); Judgment Statements and Responses; one shoebox for each two students; paint, markers, yarn, tinfoil, and other assorted art materials

Procedure

1. Introduce the Judgment Machine by showing it to the students and asking them to discuss what they think it does.

2. Demonstrate how the Judgment Machine functions by distributing the Judgment Statements to six volunteers and having them read the statements aloud to the Judgment Machine, one at a time.

3. As each volunteer reads a Judgment Statement, draw the corresponding Judgment Response from inside the Judgment Machine. Discuss.

4. As each response is being discussed, pin it up on a bulletin board in one of three categories, according to what is being judged: *Someone's Actions* (a, c, f); *Someone's Feelings* (b, e) *Someone's Appearance* (d).

5. Point out the different dimensions of our personhood that are subject to judgment. Have students brainstorm and list any other dimensions that may be judged—for example, someone's relationships or someone's lifestyle.

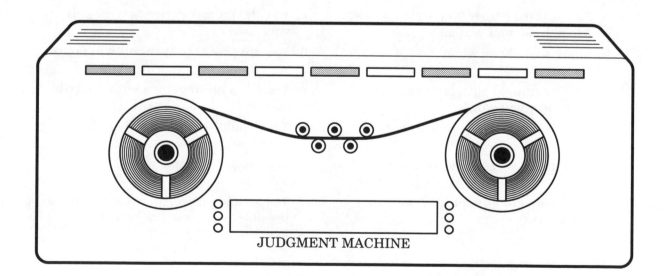

JUDGMENT MACHINE

6. Distribute one shoebox to every two students. Have students make their own Judgment Machine and, together with a partner, compose 3–4 original statements and responses like those in the examples.

7. Have students share their machines, statements, and responses upon completion.

Discussion

Content Questions

1. What did you think about the judgments?
2. What was wrong with the Judgment Machine's responses?
3. Were the judgments made by the machine fair? Why or why not?

Personalization Questions

1. Has anyone ever judged you? Share experiences.
2. How did you feel when someone did that?
3. Have you ever judged someone else?
4. What could you have done or said instead?

To the Leader

The elements that make up a judgment include a certain degree of ignorance of the facts, personal bias, and a moral connotation of some sort. These elements should be pointed out in simple terms during the content discussion so that students have a firm basis for recognizing more subtle judgmental responses when they encounter them.

Judgment Statements and Responses

Directions: Copy each statement and response on a separate index card.

a. I am a third grader, and I have a best friend in second grade.

b. I hate to do homework.

c. This morning, I got very angry and said some bad words.

d. I always wear green tennis shoes.

e. I get angry when someone ignores me.

f. I don't like to answer in class, and I hardly ever do.

a. You should make friends with kids your own age.

b. You are probably lazy and will not do well in school.

c. You are a mean person with a terrible temper.

d. You should wear white ones. You have terrible taste.

e. You are spoiled and should learn to think about others more.

f. You should answer in class as often as possible. You must not care about your schoolwork very much.

Face the Facts

Objective

To distinguish between facts and assumptions about others' behavior

Materials

Facts and Assumptions Statement Cards; old magazines; two large pieces of tagboard per small group (one labeled *Fact*, the other labeled *Assumption)*; scissors, glue, and markers as needed

Procedure

1. Display two sample advertisements, one illustrating the use of factual information in promoting a product, the other illustrating the use of suggestion, opinion, or assumption. Lead the students in an analysis and discussion of each until it is clearly established that one is based on facts that can be tested and proven and the other is based on what someone assumes or thinks about the product.

2. Pair children up and supply them with old magazines from which to cut a sample of each kind of ad. Collect the ads and, in small groups (4–6 students), have children discuss whether the examples illustrate facts or assumptions and tape them on the appropriate tagboard chart.

3. Extend the discussion of advertisements to the opinions we form of other people based on facts versus assumptions about their behavior.

4. Supply each student with a Statement Card having either a fact or assumption printed on it. Have each student read his or her statement aloud to the entire class. Discuss what category the statement belongs to, then write the statement on the chalkboard under the heading *Fact* or *Assumption.*

5. Invite students to share positive examples of facts and assumptions about another person's behavior (for example, "Andrew got glasses—now he'll always be able to see well" or "Kara got an *A*—she'll probably always get *A*'s").

Discussion

Content Questions

1. How do facts differ from assumptions?
2. How can you determine whether a statement is a fact or an assumption?
3. How are assumptions about either a product or a person inferior to facts?

Personalization Questions

1. Has anyone ever made an assumption about you?
2. How did you feel?
3. How can we avoid making assumptions?

To the Leader

The distinction between fact and assumption as based on the ability to prove or disprove the statement should be developed thoroughly. The transfer of the concept from advertisements to human behavior must be clearly articulated and reinforced or students will be confused.

Statement Cards

Directions: Copy each statement on a separate index card.

Facts

Polly is wearing a dress that is too big.

Joey does not get good grades.

Sue plays ball.

John failed a test.

Ted fell off his bike.

Ellen missed five spelling words.

Joann lives across the railroad tracks.

Sandy has a new poodle.

Billy lost his book.

Tom's parents just got a divorce.

Nate broke his leg.

Tanya plays the violin.

Assumptions

Polly always wears her sister's hand-me-downs.

Joey is stupid and lazy.

Sue will probably be the best player on the team next year.

John will never be a good student.

Ted is a terrible bike rider.

Ellen will never learn to spell a whole list of words.

All the people who live across the railroad tracks will always live there.

Just because Sandy has a new poodle, she'll think she's better.

Billy will always be irresponsible.

Tom will be upset about his parents' divorce and will never be happy again.

Nate will never run again.

Tanya will probably be a famous violinist.

Glad to Be Me

Objective

To recognize that rejection from others doesn't mean you're no good

Materials

Glad To Be Me Bookmarks (Handout 12)

Procedure

1. Retell the familiar story *The Ugly Duckling*, upgrading the language to an appropriate level for third and fourth graders.
2. Direct a large-group discussion on the moral, or lesson, of the story, using the Content Questions.
3. Have children form small groups (3–4 students) to discussion the Personalization Questions.
4. Distribute Bookmarks (Handout 12) for students to color. Collect and laminate. Punch a hole in the top of each and attach a yarn tassel to complete. Give to each student to keep.

Discussion

Content Questions

1. Why did the Ugly Duckling feel bad about himself?
2. What was faulty in the other ducklings' opinion of the Ugly Duckling's appearance?
3. Was the Ugly Duckling really ugly or just different?

Personalization Questions

1. Have you ever felt bad about who you are and wanted to be different?
2. Do other people's opinions affect how we feel about ourselves?
3. Are other people's opinions always true?

To the Leader

For this activity, Personalization Questions are to be written on the chalkboard and discussed in a small-group format.

It's Me

Objective

To examine the effects of sex stereotyping on self and others

Materials

Venn Diagram (as illustrated); pictures or words denoting traditionally male or female items and activities; It's Me Balloon Outlines (Handout 13); It's Me Bag and Baggage Cutouts (Handout 14), pint-size milk carton per student; paint, pipe cleaners, scissors, and glue as needed

Procedure

1. Display a large Venn Diagram, drawn as shown.

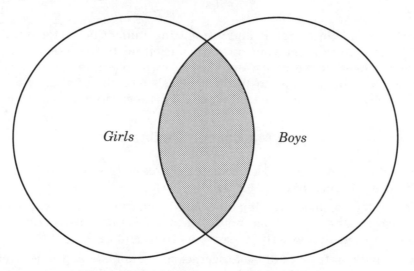

2. Display pictures or labels of items such as the following: baseball mitt, food, football helmet, bunny slippers, tools, school supplies, doll, sports car, flowers, nurse's uniform. Others items that lend themselves to sex-role stereotyping may be added or substituted. Have students vote on classification of each according to the diagram (for girls, boys, or both). Do not challenge the consensus at this point.

3. Direct a discussion based on the completed classification, using the Content Questions.

4. Distribute an It's Me Balloon Outline (Handout 13) and Bag and Baggage Cutout (Handout 14) to each student. Have students assemble the balloons and baggage as directed. Display balloons in the room.

Discussion

Content Questions

1. Why are some things thought of as being for girls? For boys?
2. Why were some items classified as belonging to both girls and boys?

3. Select two or three items from each category and challenge the students' classification—for example, is a baseball mitt necessarily always a boys' thing? Why not?

4. Just because we might expect boys and girls to do some different kinds of things, does that mean all boys and all girls must do only those things we expect them to do?

5. Is it wrong for a girl to want to do something someone else thinks is an activity for boys? For a boy to do an activity someone else thinks is for girls?

Personalization Questions

1. If you're a girl, have you ever wanted to do something that someone else said was for boys only? If you're a boy, something someone said was for girls only?

2. Does being a boy or girl ever make you feel not free to do some things you secretly want to do?

3. Is there a way you can be free in spite of what others say? What qualities must you possess as a person to do what you really want? (Stress the need for courage and strength.)

To the Leader

The group leader's attitude in modeling and influencing student behavior is an essential factor. It would be wise to examine your own attitudes prior to the lesson and to be cautious in revealing, even nonverbally, any biases to which you may still ascribe. A good follow-up activity would be listening to Marlo Thomas's recording *Free to Be . . . You and Me*, especially the selection "Mommies are People." This recording is available at public libraries.

It's Me Balloon Outline

Directions: 1. Cut down pint-size milk cartons to approximately half size. Paint and decorate to look like hot-air balloon baskets. Allow to dry.

2. Reproduce balloon drawing on colored construction paper, then cut out. When cutting out balloon, hold a second sheet of construction paper in place so shapes match exactly, to serve as front and back.

3. Glue balloon front and back together along outside edges, leaving neck and bottom margin unglued and open for stuffing. Allow to dry.

4. Decorate balloon with crayons or markers.

5. Stuff inside of balloon carefully with tissue, cotton, or any other lightweight material.

6. Attach colored pipe cleaners between precut holes in the the balloon neck and basket.

Bag and Baggage Cutout

Directions: 1. Color and cut out bags.

2. Label each bag with a few words describing something you would like to do or be.

3. Pack your balloon with your bags.

It's Me Balloon Outline

It's Me Bag and Baggage Cutout

One of a Kind

Objective

To recognize the negative effects of comparing oneself to others

Materials

Color pictures of butterflies, flowers, sunsets, puppies (two pictures of each subject); One of a Kind Butterfly Outlines (Handout 15)

Procedure

1. Project pictures on an opaque projector (or select large pictures to hold up) of two very different yet equally attractive butterflies, flowers, sunset scenes, puppies.

2. Direct a discussion of what is appealing, though different, about each of the paired pictures. Ask the students if any kind of real agreement could be reached on which one of each pair was more beautiful, better, or more valuable. If not, why not?

3. Using the Content Questions, relate the discussion of the pictures to the way we compare and evaluate people.

4. Distribute a Butterfly Outline (Handout 15) to each student. Have students create their own unique design. Cut out and share.

5. Display butterflies on the bulletin board with a caption summarizing the theme that we are all equally beautiful, though different.

Discussion

Content Questions

1. Why couldn't we adequately compare the butterflies, flowers, sunsets, or puppies and choose a best or most beautiful one?

2. If we forced a comparison and a choice, would it be really true? Would it be fair to the two things being compared? Why not?

3. Do we sometimes compare people and say some are best or more beautiful, more appealing, or more valuable? Is that true? Why or why not?

4. People have awareness, thoughts, and feelings that plants and animals do not. How do people feel when they know they are being compared to others and judged better or worse? Does feeling compared help them in any way? Does it help the people who judged them in any way?

Personalization Questions

1. Have you ever felt compared to someone else and judged to be better or worse? How did you feel?

2. How did you react when you were compared to someone else and judged? Did your behavior change from what it might have been? Was that a good change?

3. How can you resist bad feelings and negative behaviors when you find yourself unfairly judged?

4. How can you help others most when it comes to making comparisons and judgments?

5. How will it also help you to avoid making comparisons and judgments?

To the Leader

Students may say that they prefer one picture over another; if so, point out that people's preferences differ and that there is no one correct opinion as to which version is better than another.

One of a Kind Butterfly Outline

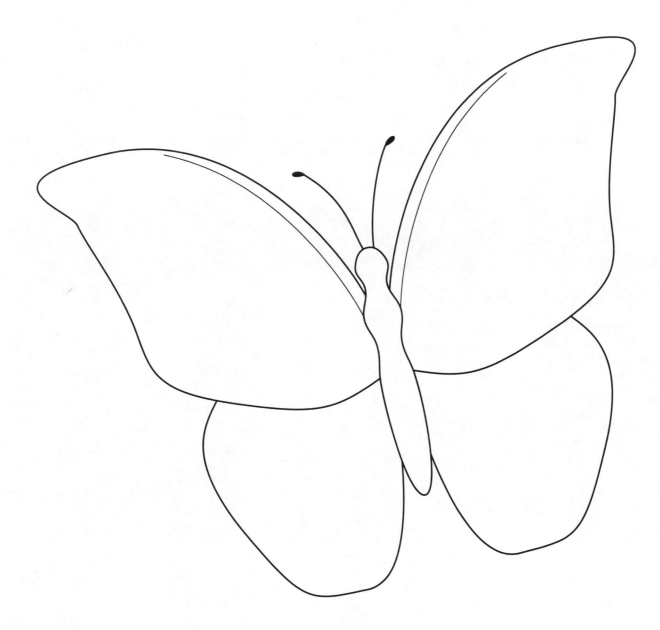

True Blue

Objective

To identify characteristics of good friendships

Materials

Blue posterboard; stencil letter patterns; markers and scissors as needed

Procedure

1. Explain that the phrase *true blue* describes a real, dependable, and lasting friendship. Discuss other kinds of phrases describing friendship (such as *fair weather, on again/off again*, etc.). Develop a definition of true blue in contrast to other kinds of friendship experiences.

2. Explain how to write simple haiku poems (most students will already have been introduced to this form in language classes). The haiku is a three-line poem in which the first line has five syllables, the second has seven, and the third has five.

   Example: True Blue

   > A friend always speaks
   > the truth, but in a soft way.
   > Kind words, gentle friend.

3. Allow students to select a partner to work with and write a haiku (or free verse poem, if they prefer) that expresses their concept of true blue friendship.

4. Have each student cut a large heart from blue poster board and copy his or her poem onto it, then decorate and display. (Use stencil lettering, if desired.)

Discussion

Content Questions

1. What distinguishes true blue friendships from other kinds?
2. What factors affect a friendship to make it true blue or not?
3. Can people work at making a friendship better, more true blue? How?

Personalization Questions

1. Have you ever had a true blue friendship? Share experiences.
2. Have you ever been disappointed by a friendship you thought was true blue but turned out not to be? Share.

To the Leader

Care must be taken in this activity to speak of the quality of the relationship and not to encourage judgment of the persons in that relationship. The choice of wording in referring to true blue friendships as opposed to true blue friends is therefore purposeful. It is important to stress that, even though not all people can become true blue friends, this fact does not reflect poorly on the people involved.

GRADES

5–6

SELF-ACCEPTANCE

Who Isn't What?

Objective

To recognize that how well a person performs doesn't make that person good or bad

Materials

Story "The Game"

Procedure

1. Introduce the activity by asking students to raise their hands to indicate whether they've ever played a game and won. Do the same for those who have ever played a game and lost.
2. Read the story, then discuss.

The Game

Sue and Sam challenged each other to a game of checkers while several other students looked on. The first few moves were fairly routine, and then suddenly Sue saw an opening and was able to gain some ground. Sam, back on the defensive, made a strategic move and had the opportunity to crown. Sue made a move, got one of Sam's checkers, and the game proceeded, neck and neck. Now the onlookers were getting nervous. Who would win this game? Sam moved . . . then Sue. Oops! Sue was cornered. But not for long! Sam made a bad play, and the game was over. Sue had won this game by a narrow margin.

Discussion

Content Questions

1. Based on the students' performance in the checker game, is it possible to know whether they're good students?
2. Based on their performance in the game, is it possible to tell whether or not they're popular?
3. Based on their performance in the game, can we determine how well they get along with brothers and sisters or parents?
4. Based on their performance in the game, do we know how well they can play checkers?
5. What do we really know about these kids?

Personalization Questions

1. Have you ever won or lost in something? Share experiences.
2. Did winning or losing make you a good or bad person or, rather, a person who won or lost a particular event? What does winning or losing tell us about who you are as a person?

3. Next time you lose at something, what can you tell yourself about the fact that you lost? (Students can tell themselves that it's just a game, that losing once doesn't mean you'll always lose, or that losing a game doesn't mean you're a loser as a person.)

To the Leader

The purpose of the lesson is to emphasize that just because you perform in a particular way doesn't mean that as a person you are good or bad. It is also important for students to realize how little can be assumed from performance at one point in time.

I Am, I Do

Objective

To recognize the relationship between self-acceptance and behavior

Materials

One index card per student; tape

Procedure

1. Write the following phrases on individual index cards: *bad kid, stupid, always in trouble, smart, never misses an answer, super friendly, "Mr. Popularity," "Miss Popularity," always chosen first, never does anything right.* (More phrases and cards may be added if more than 20 students are participating.)

2. Divide the class into two teams and invite students to participate in an experiment about labels we are assigned based on the way we behave or the way we feel about ourselves. Tape a card on the forehead of each Team 1 member. Team members should not see what is written on the card.

3. Assign each Team 1 member a Team 2 member. Each Team 2 member tries to communicate through words or actions what his or her partner's card says without stating exactly what is printed on it. (For example, the person communicating *bad kid* could say, "Can't you stay out of trouble?" or "Can't you ever be good?") Team 1 members try to guess what their labels say.

4. If desired, reverse team roles and repeat.

Discussion

Content Questions

1. Were you able to guess what your label said? If so, how were you able to do it?

2. In real life, how do you think people get labels?

Personalization Questions

1. Are you aware of having any labels that might determine how you feel about yourself or how you act? Share examples.

2. If you do have a label, how do you feel about having it? How do you think you got it?

3. Do you think that others tend to treat you in the way you're labeled?

4. If you could change your label, how would you like it to be changed?

To the Leader

It's important that students realize that how they feel about themselves is sometimes communicated through their behavior and that this in turn influences others to treat them in a particular way. Alternatively, others may label them and this in turn can influence how they feel about themselves.

Me Power

Objective

To increase students' sense of personal power by illustrating that they can solve problems

Materials

Me Power Worksheet (Handout 16); pens or pencils as needed

Procedure

1. Introduce the activity by showing students a magic wand (appropriately constructed with tinfoil, glitter, etc.). Discuss the idea of waving a magic wand to solve problems, thus gaining a sense of power over situations. Point out that, because magic wands don't really exist, we have to develop our own sense of personal power when it comes to solving problems.

2. Distribute one Me Power Worksheet (Handout 16) to each pair of students. Partners are to read each situation and come up with as many feasible solutions as possible to each problem.

Discussion

Content Questions

1. Were you able to find solutions to these problems? Share several examples of each problem.

2. How did you think of the solutions?

3. Do you think it is usually possible to think of some type of solution to almost every problem?

Personalization Questions

1. Have you ever felt as though you'd like a magic wand to solve some problem?

2. Have you used techniques like brainstorming to think of solutions because you can't magically make the situation better?

3. What can you do next time you have a problem that needs to be solved? What are some techniques that you can try?

To the Leader

Emphasize the fact that we have a lot more power than we think to solve problems or at least to make things better.

HANDOUT 16

Me Power Worksheet

Directions: Write down as many solutions as you can to the following problems.

1. Someone in your class is pressing you to take drugs.
   Solutions:

2. Someone makes fun of what you're wearing.
   Solutions:

3. You find out that your older sister drinks a lot.
   Solutions:

4. You have a big report due, and you're worried about how to write it.
   Solutions:

5. Kids are teasing you because you're in the class for gifted students.
   Solutions:

6. You're being left out of some activities during recess.
   Solutions:

Voicebox

Objective

To develop the ability to utilize positive self-talk in coping with self put-downs

Materials

Voicebox Worksheets (Handout 17); pens or pencils as needed

Procedure

1. Distribute the Voicebox Worksheets (Handout 17) and ask students if they've ever felt as if they've had a voicebox inside their heads, either urging them to do something, telling them not to do something, letting them know that they should try and are capable, or telling them that they are stupid.
2. Discuss the example on the worksheet and explain that self-talk is like a voicebox and can be positive or negative.
3. Divide students into groups of three and have them identify positive and negative self-talk for each of the situations on the worksheet.
4. Bring small groups back together to discuss the Content and Personalization Questions.

Discussion

Content Questions

1. Were you able to identify both positive and negative self-talk for each of the situations? Give an example of both kinds for each item.

Personalization Questions

1. Do you ever use self-talk?
2. Which kind do you usually use, positive or negative? Which do you think is most helpful to you?
3. What can you do the next time you hear yourself using only negative self-talk?
4. What did you learn from this activity that you can use?

To the Leader

Positive self-talk can be a powerful strategy for coping with self put-downs. Stress the importance of disputing negative messages.

Voicebox Worksheet

Directions: Identify examples of positive and negative self-talk that you might tend to use in each of the situations below. Here's an example to get you started.

Example: You are taking a test and don't do well.

If you have negative self-talk, you may be saying to yourself, "I am so stupid. I should have known those answers. Everyone is better than I am. This is awful and I'm really dumb."

If you have positive self-talk, you may be saying to yourself, "I know I didn't do well, but that doesn't mean I'm stupid. Maybe I could have studied harder, but this doesn't mean I'm dumb in everything or that I can't do better next time."

1. You strike out in a ball game.

2. You don't get a part in the school play.

3. Your best friend does better work than you do on an art project.

4. You don't get invited to a slumber party.

5. You have been having learning problems and are going to be placed in a special class.

Performance Wheel

Objective

To learn to differentiate between poor performance in one area and being a complete failure

Materials

Performance Wheels; Performance Wheel Worksheets (Handout 18); pens or pencils as needed

Procedure

1. Divide students into small groups (3–4 participants). Distribute a Performance Wheel and Performance Wheel Worksheet (Handout 18) to each group and explain that the activity deals with doing well and not doing well in the various categories identified on the wheel.

2. Have one student in the group spin the wheel and, on the worksheet, identify a time he or she did very well on a task associated with that particular category (for example, in the category music, memorizing a solo without making a mistake). Have the same student spin again, this time identifying a situation associated with this particular category in which he or she did quite poorly (for example, in the category sports, losing a game).

3. Instruct other students in each group to take turns spinning until all categories have been covered. (If the spinner lands on the same category twice, spin again.)

Discussion

Content Questions

1. What was it like to think of things you did well and not so well in the various categories?
2. Were some categories more difficult to think of examples for than other areas?
3. Were some of the examples shared by group members similar to situations you've experienced?

Personalization Questions

1. If you did well in some categories and not in others, what does that mean?
2. Do you think it is possible to achieve in all categories all the time?
3. What did you learn from this activity that you can apply to your life?

To the Leader

As students share their experiences, they learn that individuals have areas in which they excel and areas in which they don't. Emphasize the importance of understanding that poor performance in one or more areas doesn't make a person a total failure.

Performance Wheel

Directions: Make Performance Wheels from poster board or other heavy paper. Use a brass brad in the center to attach the spinner.

Performance Wheel Worksheet

Directions: As you spin the wheel and land on a category, identify a time when you did quite well in that area. Spin again and identify a time when you did not do so well. After two spins, let another student take a turn.

	Did Well	**Not So Well**
1. Leadership	_____	_____
2. Making friends	_____	_____
3. Math	_____	_____
4. Music	_____	_____
5. Sports	_____	_____
6. Doing chores	_____	_____
7. Following rules	_____	_____
8. Swimming	_____	_____
9. Listening	_____	_____

Accept or Change

Objective

To learn which aspects of self can be changed and which need to be accepted

Materials

Accept or Change Worksheets (Handout 19); pens or pencils as needed

Procedure

1. Introduce the activity by distributing the Accept or Change Worksheets (Handout 19) and explaining that students will have an opportunity to determine which aspects of themselves they can or cannot change.
2. Have students mark the continuum for each item on the worksheet.

Discussion

Content Questions

1. Count the number of items that you thought you couldn't change. Now count the items you thought you could change. Which category has more items?
2. What are some examples of things that you think you have no control over? Some degree of control, but not much? A lot of control?
3. Do you think you can effect some change in most areas or not? What sorts of things might you have to do to change your relationships with friends or your attitude, for example?

Personalization Questions

1. What can you do about those areas over which you have no control?
2. Have you ever told yourself that you can't change a situation when, in fact, you really could to some extent if you did some things differently?
3. What can you do next time you think you can't change something?

To the Leader

Oftentimes, we don't realize what our options are or try to modify our behavior to effect change. Help students see, for example, that by changing what they eat they can change their weight, or by smiling and saying "Hi" they might make changes in their friendships. Also stress that certain things won't change, and we simply need to accept them.

HANDOUT 19

Accept or Change Worksheet

Directions: Read each item below and decide how much you are able to change it. Put a mark on the continuum to show how much control you think you have.

	Can't change at all	**Can totally change**
1. Nose	├────────────────────────────┤	
2. Height	├────────────────────────────┤	
3. Weight	├────────────────────────────┤	
4. Skin color	├────────────────────────────┤	
5. Grades	├────────────────────────────┤	
6. Attitude	├────────────────────────────┤	
7. Relationships with teachers	├────────────────────────────┤	
8. Relationships with parents	├────────────────────────────┤	
9. Color of hair	├────────────────────────────┤	
10. Style of clothes	├────────────────────────────┤	
11. Age	├────────────────────────────┤	
12. Relationships with friends	├────────────────────────────┤	

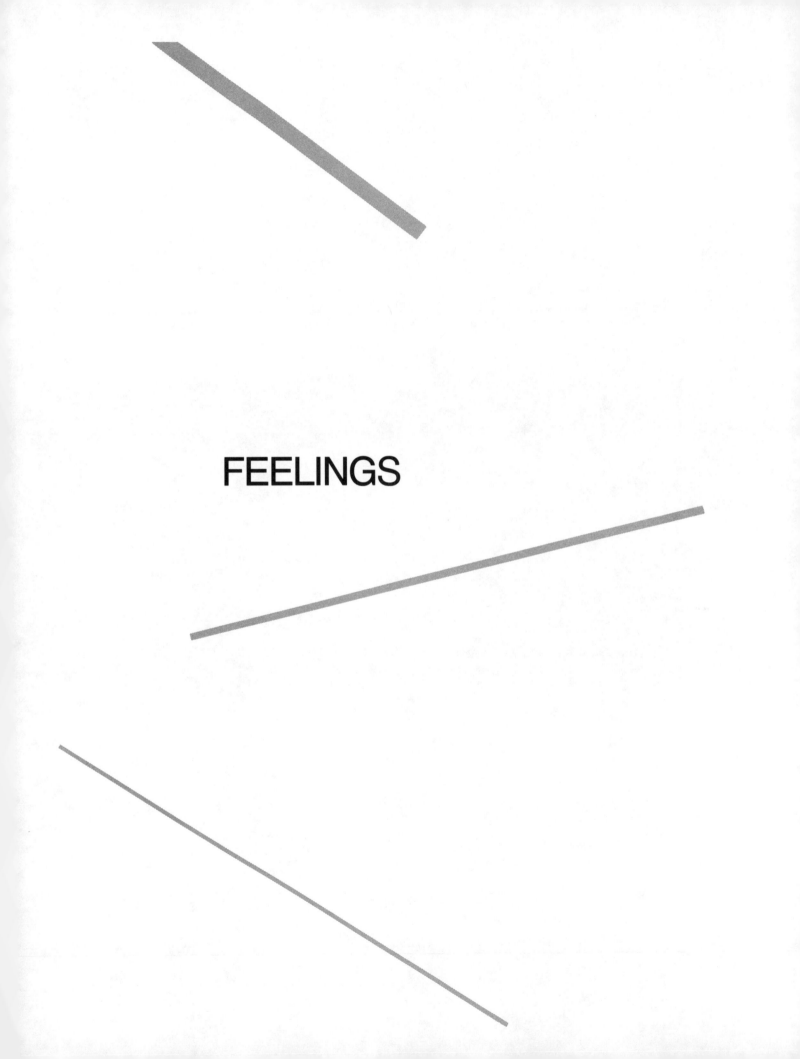

FEELINGS

They Made Me Feel

Objective

To learn that others don't control your feelings or make you feel a certain way

Materials

They Made Me Feel Situations; eight pieces of string

Procedure

1. Ask for a volunteer to be "It" and eight other volunteers to read the They Made Me Feel Situations. Attach the strings to the arms, legs, and fingers of the volunteer who is "It."

2. Ask the first reader volunteer to take hold of one of the strings, read the first situation, identify what the feeling associated with that situation is, and then pull on the string. Other volunteers are to do the same. When all the situations have been read, the volunteers may sit down.

Discussion

Content Questions

1. To the "It" volunteer: How did you feel when the people were telling how you would feel in the situation and "pulling your strings?" Did it seem as though they were making you feel a certain way?

2. Would it be possible to feel more than one way in the situations given? In other words, do you have a choice about what to feel?

Personalization Questions

1. Have you ever said someone made you mad (or sad, upset, etc.)? What do you mean when you say that?

2. Do you think others can really make you feel something, or do you choose the way you feel?

3. The next time you hear someone saying, "He or she makes me so mad," what will you think?

To the Leader

Our language is replete with references that suggest other people make us feel some way. Children need to learn that to feel is their choice.

They Made Me Feel Situations

She called me a name.

He pushed me off the slide at recess.

My mom yelled at me.

My brother teased me in front of my friends.

My sister wouldn't let me watch my favorite TV show.

I failed a test.

I had to re-do work in language arts.

I didn't get invited to a skating party.

Help or Hinder?

Objective

To learn that some feelings help and some hinder

Materials

Individual strips of paper, labeled with the specified feeling words

Procedure

1. Label individual strips of paper with the following feeling words: *loved, afraid, worried, sad, patient, confused, scared, angry, hurt, embarrassed, jealous, ashamed, frightened, excited, mixed up, guilty, mean, comfortable, moody, discouraged, frustrated, brave, awful, sensitive, terrible, gloomy, helpless, bad, different, happy, elated, hateful,* and *depressed.* Make enough so that each group of four students has one complete set of words.

2. Divide students into groups of four and distribute the sets of feeling words. Discuss the concept of feelings that help versus feelings that hinder. Feelings that help are ones we usually like to experience; they energize us and result in positive things. Feelings that hinder are ones that result in negative relationships with others, negative feelings toward self, bad moods, or perhaps even troublesome behavior.

3. Ask groups to sort the words into piles labeled *Help* or *Hinder.* If students believe the feelings could go either way, they could start a third pile, labeled *Help and Hinder.* Encourage sharing of experiences as students do the sorting.

4. When the task is completed, list on the chalkboard under the headings *Help* and *Hinder* all words for which there is consensus. Those for which there is no consensus can be placed in the third category.

Discussion

Content Questions

1. Which list has more words—*Help* or *Hinder*?
2. Were some words more difficult than others to categorize? Why do you think this was the case?
3. What do you think distinguishes helpful feelings from those that hinder?

Personalization Questions

1. Which type of feelings do you generally experience? Which do you want to experience?
2. Do you like having feelings that hinder? If not, can you do anything about them?

To the Leader

Helping students differentiate between kinds of feelings develops awareness that hindering feelings may be avoided or dealt with in a way different from helping feelings.

Healthy/Unhealthy Expression

Objective

To learn to distinguish between healthy and unhealthy expression of feelings

Materials

Healthy/Unhealthy Expression Worksheets (Handout 20); pens or pencils as needed

Procedure

1. Discuss the difference between healthy and unhealthy expression of feelings. For example, if a person were angry, unhealthy expression would be throwing something and breaking it, whereas healthy expression would be talking about the problem without exploding. Invite students to share a few additional examples.
2. Ask students to find a partner and give each pair a Healthy/Unhealthy Expression Worksheet (Handout 20). Partners are to work together to fill in the worksheet.
3. After students complete the worksheet, have several pairs share examples of healthy and unhealthy expression for selected feelings. Record all suggestions on the chalkboard under the headings *Healthy Expression* and *Unhealthy Expression*.

Discussion

Content Questions

1. Was it more difficult to think of healthy or unhealthy ways to express the feelings?
2. Were some feelings more difficult than others to find ways to express?

Personalization Questions

1. Do you usually express your feelings in healthy or unhealthy ways?
2. If you do practice unhealthy ways, can you do anything about that? Have you ever changed the way in which you have expressed feelings?
3. Do you see any payoffs from unhealthy expressions of emotions?
4. Do you see any advantages to healthy expression? What can you do to increase healthy expression?

To the Leader

The distinction between these two types of expression is particularly important because children who practice healthy expression will also be more emotionally healthy in general.

HANDOUT 20

Healthy/Unhealthy Expression Worksheet

Directions: Identify healthy and unhealthy ways to express each of the following feelings.

	Healthy	Unhealthy
1. Anger		
2. Disappointment		
3. Fear		
4. Worry		
5. Sadness		

Changing Thoughts, Changing Feelings

Objective

To recognize how feelings change when thoughts change

Materials

Two boxes, one labeled *Feelings*, the other labeled *Thoughts*; Changing Thoughts, Changing Feelings Worksheets (Handout 21); pens or pencils and scissors as needed

Procedure

1. Discuss the difference between thoughts and feelings about an event. Give an example, such as losing a game. At first, you might feel ashamed or angry, and you might be thinking that you were clumsy or incompetent or that the other team cheated. But, when you have calmed down and as time goes by, even though you might still feel bad about losing, you may realize that you played quite well, that the other team just had more strength, etc. Elicit some additional examples from students.

2. Distribute the Changing Thoughts, Changing Feelings Worksheets (Handout 21) and have students identify a feeling for each of the situations. In addition, they are to write down what they would likely be thinking about the situation.

3. Ask three students to cut off the answers to Situation 1 and separate the columns so that one section contains a feeling, one a thought. They are to put these in the appropriate boxes.

4. Draw out each of the feelings and compare them. Are all the feelings the same? Then draw out the corresponding thoughts. Are all the thoughts the same? Discuss alternate thoughts that could exist about each event and decide whether or not the feeling would change if the thought changed. (This may be evident from the different responses of the three students.)

5. Continue this procedure with three new volunteers each for Situations 2, 3, and 4.

Discussion

Content Questions

1. Was it difficult to identify thoughts associated with feelings about an event?

2. What difference does it make when you change your thoughts about a situation? How does this affect your feelings?

Personalization Questions

1. Have you ever changed your feelings because you changed your thoughts? Share situations and examples.

2. If you wanted to change your thoughts and feelings, how would you go about doing so?

3. What have you learned about thoughts and feelings?

To the Leader

Students who become adept at changing their thoughts are better able to deal with their emotions. It is important to help students see that putting some distance between themselves and the situation often results in less intense emotions and less negative thinking.

Changing Thoughts, Changing Feelings Worksheet

Directions: Read each of the situations. Then, in the blanks below the line, identify how you would feel and what you might be thinking about each of the situations.

Situation 1
Your best friend is going on vacation and says that he or she will send you a postcard. You don't get the card.

Situation 2
You are selected for the All Stars Baseball Team. The game begins in a few minutes.

Situation 3
You are invited to a party, but you don't want to go because you don't like the kid who is giving it. Your mom says you should go.

Situation 4
You wanted a new dress for the school music program. Your mother picked it out, and now you have to wear it even if you hate it and feel like a nerd in it.

Situation 1 Feeling	Situation 1 Thoughts
_____	_____ _____ _____
Situation 2 Feeling	Situation 2 Thoughts
_____	_____ _____ _____
Situation 3 Feeling	Situation 3 Thoughts
_____	_____ _____ _____
Situation 4 Feeling	Situation 4 Thoughts
_____	_____ _____ _____

How Might They Feel?

Objective

To learn to identify how others might be feeling in order to encourage sensitivity

Materials

Paper and pencils as needed; a newspaper clipping for each student (these should describe a broad range of events: illnesses, fires, and accidents; honors and awards; theatrical events, concerts, and speeches; births and graduations; etc.)

Procedure

1. Ask students what they think it means to be sensitive to someone else's feelings. Discuss the importance of putting yourself in someone else's place and imagining how you might feel if you found yourself in a certain situation.

2. Distribute the newspaper clippings. Ask students to read the clippings and write down as many feeling words as necessary to describe the emotions of the people involved. If there are several different perspectives represented, ask students to identify the various people's feelings. (For example, a young violinist giving a performance might feel nervous, whereas his or her parents might feel proud.)

3. Invite students to share their clippings and explain what they think the person(s) might be feeling.

Discussion

Content Questions

1. How difficult was it to figure out how the other person(s) might be feeling?

2. Was it more difficult to identify what others were feeling in some of the situations that were shared? What do you think accounts for the difference?

3. Do you think you know for sure how the people in these situations feel? Why or why not?

Personalization Questions

1. Have you ever been in a situation in which you thought you knew how someone was feeling and were wrong? Share examples.

2. What are some clues that you can use in order to be sensitive to how someone else might feel?

3. Is there anything you can do to find out exactly how another person feels?

To the Leader

Although it is never possible to know exactly how someone else is feeling, students can read body language, ask the person directly, or project themselves into the other person's situation.

Feelings and Physical Reactions

Objective

To learn to recognize the connection between feelings and physical reactions

Materials

Life-size outline of a body, traced on paper

Procedure

1. Engage students in a short brainstorming activity in which they are to think of as many feeling words as they can. List these on the chalkboard.

2. Hang up the body outline and explain that, when we have an emotion, we also usually have a bodily response. (For example, when we feel happy, we may feel like jumping or running.)

3. Have students identify what they feel like doing or what bodily sensations they have when they experience the various feelings listed on the board. For example:

   When I am sad, my chest feels tight.

   When I am scared, I have sweaty hands and a queasy stomach.

   When I am mad, my face feels hot.

4. Write the feeling words on the appropriate part of the body outline as students describe their responses.

5. Review the concept presented in earlier activities that, if you change your thoughts about a situation, your feelings will also very likely change. Changing your thoughts can also therefore affect the bodily sensations associated with feelings. For instance, you could change your thoughts about how awful it would be if you make a mistake on a test, thus reducing your anxiety. With less anxiety, you would probably not experience sweaty palms, butterflies in the stomach, etc.

Discussion

Content Questions

1. When you have a feeling, do you have some choice about your physical reaction?
2. Do you think physical reactions are good or bad?

Personalization Questions

1. Which bodily reactions do you experience the most?
2. Do you usually have more physical reactions when you experience positive or negative feelings?
3. Which physical reactions would you like to increase? Which would you like to eliminate?
4. What do you think you can do to change physical reactions?

To the Leader

It is important to review the relationship between thoughts and feelings and to stress that students can have some control over bodily reactions by changing their thoughts and decreasing the intensity of negative emotion.

BELIEFS AND BEHAVIOR

Rational or Irrational

Objective

To learn to distinguish between rational and irrational beliefs

Materials

Rational or Irrational Beliefs List (Handout 22)

Procedure

1. Introduce the activity by writing the words *rational* and *irrational* on the chalkboard. Explain that irrational beliefs don't make good sense, whereas rational beliefs do. For example, demanding that your mother fix fried chicken every Sunday is irrational; merely wishing that she would but realizing that she may not is rational. Believing that everyone in the school is mean is irrational; realizing that only one or two people act mean some of the time is rational.

2. Discuss why the following statements are irrational beliefs.

    I must be perfect.

    Everyone should always like me all of the time.

    I can't help the way I feel; it's someone else's fault if I'm unhappy.

    It's awful if everything doesn't always go the way I want it to.

    I shouldn't have to work too hard at anything.

    I can't make mistakes.

    I can't stand to be criticized.

    Everyone and everything in this world should be fair.

3. Divide students into two teams, then appoint one player per team to be the captain. Give each team a Rational or Irrational Beliefs List (Handout 22). The game proceeds as follows: The captain of Team 1 reads the first statement on the list to his or her first player, who decides whether the statement is rational or irrational. If the player is correct, he or she remains standing. If not, the player sits down. Team 2 then gets a turn. The captain of Team 2 reads the next statement to the first player on his or her team. That player says whether the statement is rational or irrational, sitting down if the response is incorrect. The game continues with teams taking turns and team captains allowing members to respond in order until all of the questions have been answered. At the end of the game, the team who has the most players still standing is the winner.

Discussion

Content Questions

1. Was it difficult to distinguish between rational and irrational thoughts? Were some more difficult than others?

2. How would you explain to someone the difference between these two kinds of beliefs?

Personalization Questions

1. Do you tend to have more rational or irrational beliefs?
2. What kind of irrational beliefs do you have? Share examples.

To the Leader

Beliefs are irrational if they are demanding, absolutistic, or overgeneralized. For instance, although it would be preferable for most people to be nice to us most of the time, it is impossible for *all* people to be nice to us *all* of the time. Understanding the difference between rational and irrational thinking will enable students to recognize patterns in their own lives.

Rational or Irrational Beliefs Answer Key

1. Irrational
2. Irrational
3. Rational
4. Irrational
5. Irrational
6. Irrational

7. Rational
8. Irrational
9. Rational
10. Irrational
11. Rational
12. Irrational

13. Rational
14. Irrational
15. Rational
16. Irrational
17. Irrational
18. Rational

HANDOUT 22

Rational or Irrational Beliefs List

1. I've never had any friends.

2. No one ever asks me to go anywhere.

3. I wish I could have a new stereo.

4. If I can't go to the skating party, I'll die.

5. If she is really my friend, she should always sit by me and not by other kids.

6. My parents never let me do anything.

7. It would be nice if he would invite me to stay overnight, but just because he hasn't, that doesn't mean he doesn't like me.

8. I'm such a terrible basketball player. If I go out onto that floor, everyone will laugh and make fun of me.

9. If I make a mistake on this test, it doesn't mean I'm a dummy.

10. Everyone should say nice things to me.

11. I wish I had more friends.

12. If I have to sit next to him, I might as well quit school.

13. I really don't like her, but if I have to be her partner I guess I can stand it.

14. Just because I lost in arm wrestling, everyone is going to make fun of me and call me a wimp.

15. If my mom yells at me, it just means she's had a bad day, not that she doesn't love me.

16. There's no way I can wear my sister's hand-me-down clothes to school. Everyone will make fun of the way I look.

17. If I have to be in a class with those kids, I might as well quit school.

18. I would like to go skiing over spring break like some of the other kids, but I understand my parents can't afford it.

It's Always

Objective

To identify examples and effects of overgeneralized thinking

Materials

None

Procedure

1. Explain that this activity uses a voting strategy in which students are to respond by raising their hands high if they agree with the statement you read and by putting their hands down if they disagree. If they are in the middle, they can raise their hands halfway.

2. Read the following statements.

> All fifth graders are good readers.
>
> All girls like to cook.
>
> All boys are strong.
>
> No one in our class can play an instrument well.
>
> All people who live in big houses are rich.
>
> Everyone who has long hair smokes cigarettes.
>
> All sixth graders are good athletes.

Discussion

Content Questions

1. Was it easy to decide whether you agreed or disagreed with these statements?
2. How did the words *all*, *no one*, and *everyone* complicate the questions?
3. To overgeneralize means that you lump everything or everyone into one big category and assume that what applies to one applies to all. Do you think that the statements we read are examples of overgeneralizations?
4. What is the effect of overgeneralization? Does it cause any problems, or is it a good way to think?

Personalization Questions

1. Have you ever overgeneralized? Share examples.
2. Next time you catch yourself thinking this way, what can you do to change?

To the Leader

Encourage students to challenge the overgeneralizations. A good strategy for students to apply if they find themselves overgeneralizing is to ask themselves if the statement really applies to everyone, all the time, without exception.

Shoulds, Shoulds, Shoulds

Objective

To identify examples and effects of absolutistic thinking patterns involving shoulds, musts, and oughts

Materials

Paper and pencils as needed

Procedure

1. Review the concept of irrational thinking from Grades 5–6 Beliefs and Behavior Activity 1 (Rational or Irrational). Emphasize the fact that a good deal of irrational thinking relates to *shoulds* that we have about how an event should occur, how someone should act, or how we ourselves should be. List the following examples on the chalkboard.

    I should always be a good teacher and never lose my temper with children.

    People should always act the way I want them to.

    I should be able to buy everything I want.

2. Ask students to get out paper and pencil and think of some of the *shoulds* they have for themselves or for other people. Encourage them to think about times that they have been upset with themselves or others because they believed something should be a certain way.

3. Invite students to share some of their examples. List these on the board.

4. Discuss the feelings and consequences that result from this kind of thinking. For example, you may feel upset and get into an argument with your friend if you think he or she should do something your way.

Discussion

Content Questions

1. Do you think you have a lot of "shouldy" thinking?
2. Do you think that the feelings that result from this kind of thinking are good or not so good?
3. Are the consequences of this kind of thinking good or not so good?

Personalization Questions

1. If you have a lot of this kind of thinking, would you or would you not like to change it?
2. What are some of the consequences you have experienced as a result of this kind of thinking?

To the Leader

Helping children assess the negative feelings and consequences that result from absolutistic thinking is a necessary step in developing strategies for change.

Rose-Colored Glasses

Objective

To identify the effects of irrational thinking

Materials

Two pairs of glasses, one with lenses covered in black construction paper and the other in pink; Rose-Colored Glasses Worksheets (Handout 23); pens or pencils as needed

Procedure

1. Introduce the idea of looking at things through rose-colored glasses, which means that everything looks great. Explain that if we hold onto "shouldy" and irrational thoughts, we may act as though we are looking at things through black glasses instead. This means looking at things negatively, and looking at things negatively can affect the way we feel and behave.

2. Have students pair up, then distribute Rose-Colored Glasses Worksheet (Handout 23) to each pair.

3. Ask for two volunteers to put on the glasses. Have a third volunteer read the first situation on the list aloud and the negative belief associated with it. The student with the black glasses on is to tell how he or she would feel and act based on this negative (irrational) perspective. The student with the rose-colored glasses on is then to state the more positive (rational) belief and answer the same questions from this new perspective.

4. Instruct students to work together to fill out the rest of the sheet. Share responses when complete.

Discussion

Content Questions

1. Do you see a difference between the effects of rational and irrational thinking? What is this difference?

2. Which kind of thinking results in a more positive effect?

Personalization Questions

1. Which kind of thinking do you typically practice?

2. What have your experiences been with the effects of irrational thinking?

3. Do you want to change anything about the way you think? If so, what?

To the Leader

Reinforce the difference between the effects of rational and irrational thinking, pointing out that irrational thinking does result in more negative feelings and behaviors.

HANDOUT 23

Rose-Colored Glasses Worksheet

Directions: Read each situation. First, read the irrational belief and pretend that you have on your black glasses. Now write down how you might feel and act. Next, read the rational belief and imagine that you have on your rose-colored glasses. Again, write down how you might feel and act.

1. Your best friend does not sit by you during lunch.
   Irrational: A good friend should always do what I want him or her to do.

   How I might feel　　　　　　　**How I might act**

   _____　　　_____

   _____　　　_____

   Rational: Just because my friend doesn't sit next to me, that doesn't mean he or she doesn't like me.

   How I might feel　　　　　　　**How I might act**

   _____　　　_____

   _____　　　_____

2. Your mom won't let you invite a particular friend to stay overnight.
   Irrational: She should let me invite whomever I want.

   How I might feel　　　　　　　**How I might act**

   _____　　　_____

   _____　　　_____

   Rational: It would be nice if she'd let me invite whom I want, but there's no reason she has to.

   How I might feel　　　　　　　**How I might act**

   _____　　　_____

   _____　　　_____

Rose-Colored Glasses Worksheet

3. You don't get a good grade on a paper.
   Irrational: I'm smart and I should always get good grades.

   How I might feel **How I might act**

   _____ _____

   _____ _____

   Rational: Even though I'm smart I don't always get good grades.

   How I might feel **How I might act**

   _____ _____

   _____ _____

4. Someone calls you chicken because you won't try smoking a cigarette.
   Irrational: This person shouldn't force me to do things; it makes it impossible for me to know what to do . . . risk friendships or do something I don't want to.

   How I might feel **How I might act**

   _____ _____

   _____ _____

   Rational: I wish they wouldn't pressure me, but I have choices even if they're hard ones.

   How I might feel **How I might act**

   _____ _____

   _____ _____

5. Your sister refuses to do her share of the chores, and you get blamed for it.
   Irrational: It's not fair that I get blamed when I didn't do anything wrong.

   How I might feel **How I might act**

   _____ _____

   _____ _____

   Rational: It really isn't right, but sometimes parents make mistakes, too.

   How I might feel **How I might act**

   _____ _____

   _____ _____

Consequences

Objective

To recognize short- and long-term consequences of behavior

Materials

Story "Consequences"; paper and pencils as needed

Procedure

1. Discuss the meaning of the word *consequence*, indicating that situations have both short- and long-term consequences. For example, the short-term consequence of studying may be getting good grades. The long-term consequence may be getting into college or getting a good job.

2. Read the story, then have students make a list of the short- and long-term consequences exemplified in it.

Consequences

Aaron called Lyle and asked him to go to a movie Saturday night, stating that Aaron's dad would drive them to the theater and then pick them up after the movie. Lyle was excited about going.

When Aaron and Lyle got to the theater, Aaron waited until his dad had pulled out of the parking lot, and then he told Lyle that he didn't really want to see the movie but had just used it as an excuse so they could go a few blocks up the street to the arcade. Lyle was hesitant because he knew his mom would never let him to go the arcade, but he didn't want to disappoint Aaron, so he said he would go.

The arcade was packed when they got there, and there were lots of older kids hanging around. Aaron acted as if he knew some of them and walked off, pretty much ignoring Lyle. Lyle felt very uncomfortable.

Pretty soon, Aaron came up with a couple of other kids and told Lyle to follow him. They went outside to a car, where Aaron and the other kids each lit up a cigarette. They kept pushing Lyle to take one too, and he finally did. He didn't like the taste, but he didn't want the other kids to think he was chicken to try it.

They sat in the car quite a while, and finally Aaron said they should go back to the movie theater. When they got there, Aaron's dad was furious. He had been waiting for them in the lobby. On top of it, he smelled smoke on the boys' breath. He told Aaron he certainly couldn't be trusted and that he was going to have to tell Lyle's mom what had happened.

Discussion

Content Questions

1. What were the short-term consequences of the boys' behavior?
2. What were the long-term consequences?

3. How are these kinds of consequences related?

4. When should you think of the consequences of behavior? Why?

Personalization Questions

1. Are you aware of short- and long-term consequences in your own life? Share some examples.

2. Do you usually think of consequences before you act or after? Which do you think helps you more? What can you do to help yourself think ahead?

To the Leader

The short-term consequence in the story would likely be that Lyle is punished. The long-term consequence might be that Lyle wouldn't be able to stand up for what he thought was right in the future. This inability could lead to more negative behavior, a poor reputation, or even an addiction.

Erase the Irrational

Objective

To develop strategies for challenging irrational beliefs in self or others

Materials

Erase the Irrational Worksheets (Handout 24); pens or pencils as needed

Procedure

1. Hold up an eraser and elicit ideas about its purpose (essentially, to get rid of or replace something).
2. Have students pair up. Distribute one Erase the Irrational Worksheet (Handout 24) per pair. Indicate that students are to read each of the irrational beliefs and "erase" it by replacing it with a rational one. For example, an irrational belief might be that you should always get a part if you try out for a play. The rational belief would be that sometimes you will and sometimes you won't—but there's nothing that says you always should.
3. Have students share examples of the rational beliefs they replaced for the irrational ones.

Discussion

Content Questions

1. What do you see as the difference between rational and irrational beliefs?
2. What do you need to do in order to erase and replace irrational beliefs?

Personalization Questions

1. Have you ever applied this process of erasing and replacing beliefs? If so, what was the process like?
2. If you haven't erased and replaced irrational beliefs before, why might you want to do so? How would you go about accomplishing this?
3. What have you learned from this activity that you might be able to apply to your life?

To the Leader

Although challenging irrational beliefs is a difficult process, students can be taught to ask themselves questions that redirect their thinking. Supplying them with several examples will help them learn the process.

HANDOUT 24

Erase the Irrational Worksheet

Irrational Belief   **Rational Belief**

1. I should be perfect in everything.

   1. _____

       _____

2. My friends should always do what I want them to.

   2. _____

       _____

3. If I make a mistake, I'm dumb.

   3. _____

       _____

4. Everyone should like me.

   4. _____

       _____

5. I'm the only one around the house who ever does any work.

   5. _____

       _____

6. The way I'm working on my project is the best way, and others should do it my way.

   6. _____

       _____

7. I shouldn't have to go out of my way to make friends. People should come to me.

   7. _____

       _____

8. It's not my fault that I'm unhappy all the time.

   8. _____

       _____

9. Other kids shouldn't just stand there during a game—they should put in as much effort as I do.

   9. _____

       _____

10. My friends should always listen to what I have to say.

   10. _____

        _____

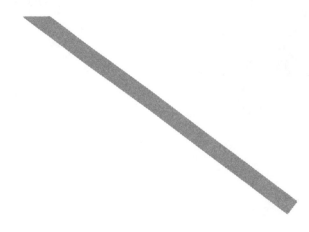

PROBLEM SOLVING/
DECISION MAKING

Approach or Avoid

Objective

To learn to differentiate between approach and avoidance problem-solving/decision-making strategies

Materials

Approach or Avoid Problem Situations

Procedure

1. Select two students to role play the following reactions to a typical problem.

   A student receives a poor grade on a test, hides the paper in her room, and goes out with friends without telling her parent(s).

   A student receives a poor grade on a test and gives it to his parent(s), saying, "I guess we'll have to talk about this."

2. Direct a discussion of the two different reactions to the problem. Why did the students react as they did? Was one way better than the other? Which one? Why?

3. Explain the terms *approach* and *avoidance* as being two different reactions to any problem. Approaching a problem means that you deal with it by talking it out, admitting that it is a problem, etc. Avoiding a problem means that you try to deny it, perhaps lie, blame it on someone else, etc.

4. Invite volunteers to role play approach and avoidance reactions to the Approach or Avoid Problem Situations. Discuss the situations following each role play.

Discussion

Content Questions

1. Why is avoidance not an effective technique for solving problems?
2. Why do people not always approach problems?
3. What are some common avoidance behaviors kids use? How are those behaviors harmful?
4. What are some approach behaviors that can be used instead?

Personalization Questions

1. Have you ever avoided a problem? How did you feel about this kind of reaction? Share examples.
2. Have you ever approached a problem? How did you feel about this kind of reaction? Share examples.
3. Is there a problem you are avoiding at present? How can you approach it to get it resolved?

To the Leader

Many children are victims of problems they cannot solve. In some instances, avoidance behavior is an effective coping mechanism. It should be pointed out that there may be times to avoid instead of approach. The distinction should also be made, however, between coping with problems and resolving them. As a means towards resolution, avoidance is usually ineffective.

Approach or Avoid Problem Situations

You receive a detention for cutting class. You have to have your parent(s) sign the detention slip.

Your teacher gave you an extra day to turn in your homework, but you still don't have it finished.

You have to choose between your mom or dad to spend your holidays with.

Your best friend has been acting distant and avoiding you lately.

The prinicipal has asked you to come to the office after school.

You are really irritated by the way a certain friend always teases you about your clothes.

Assess the Decision

Objective

To develop skills to assess what makes a decision good or bad

Materials

Assess the Decision Forms (Handout 25); paper and pencils as needed

Procedure

1. Discuss what's involved in making good versus bad decisions. In doing so, emphasize each of the following concepts: short-term consequences, long-term consequences, effects on self, effects on other people, time considerations, money/resource considerations, potential positive possibilities, and potential negative possibilities.

2. Divide students into small groups (4–6 participants) to devise a form to use in evaluating decisions. Distribute the Assess the Decision Form (Handout 25) as a model, if desired.

3. Upon completion, have students display and explain the forms they have created. Ask the whole class to work together to complete each group's form, using sample decisions suggested by the leader. These might include deciding whether or not to continue playing in a band you don't like very well, to accept an invitation from someone who isn't "in," or to start working on a report due next week or go skating with a friend.

4. Encourage students to make a form of some sort for their individual use, employing some of the ideas shared by the small groups.

Discussion

Content Questions

1. What factors must be considered in evaluating a decision you've made?

2. What are some ways to keep track of all the factors or aspects of a decision to be evaluated?

Personalization Questions

1. What decision have you made that you consider good? What made that decision good?

2. What decision have you made that you consider bad? What made that decision bad?

3. Can you change a bad decision to a good one by altering one or two factors?

To the Leader

Evaluating decisions is a difficult analytical process. Students may need further practice and reinforcement in looking at the factors involved and in understanding the many aspects of a single decision. Follow-up lessons will probably be necessary.

Assess the Decision Form

Effects on Me

_____

_____

_____

_____

Short-term Effects

_____

_____

_____

Time Required

_____

_____

_____

Positive Possibilities (Future)

_____

_____

_____

Effects on Others

_____

_____

_____

_____

Long-term Effects

_____

_____

_____

Money/Resources Needed

_____

_____

_____

Negative Possibilities (Future)

_____

_____

_____

Yours vs. Mine vs. Ours

Objective

To recognize that compromise is part of decision making

Materials

Paper and pencils as needed

Procedure

1. Assign students to small groups (4–6 participants) and give each group a list of three projects or activities they could do based on one of the content areas they are currently studying.

2. Direct each group to decide on one project that they might work on together.

3. Ask groups to tell what project they chose. Discuss the process used in deciding: How did they reach their group decision? Was there any disagreement? How was it handled?

4. Ask the students to consider what would have happened if everyone in the group disagreed and no one would give in. Have students share stories of personal experiences with such standoffs. Stress that compromise is an essential part of group decision making.

5. Have students compose a poem using the letters of the word *compromise* to begin each line. For example:

> C ooperation among people is essential.
>
> O nly when we work together can we achieve.
>
> M any ideas are better than one.
>
> P
>
> R
>
> O
>
> M
>
> I
>
> S
>
> E

Discussion

Content Questions

1. What is compromise?
2. When is compromise essential? Appropriate?
3. Is it ever wrong to compromise? When?
4. What positive or negative things result from compromising?

Personalization Questions

1. Are there times that you are stubborn or willful? What effect does behavior of this type have on the outcome of situations?

2. What kinds of things have you compromised about? How did compromising make you feel? Share examples.

To the Leader

Compromise must be viewed as a positive behavior only when and where it is appropriate and beneficial. It is not desirable for a student to compromise when, for example, he or she is being pressured by peers to engage in a dangerous or nonproductive behavior. This idea should be explained to students and reinforced regularly in the context of daily classroom occurrences.

If I Say So

Objective

To develop the ability to use rational thinking skills for problem management

Materials

Assorted construction or art paper; colored pens, pencils, and markers; laminating materials

Procedure

1. Review the concept of rational and irrational beliefs from Grades 5–6 Beliefs and Behavior Activity 1 (Rational or Irrational). Discuss the effect of self-talk on one's feelings and behavior.

2. Relate rational and irrational beliefs to the decision-making process. Share an example, such as saying to yourself before giving a report or performance, "I may make a fool of myself, but at least I'll know I've tried." Elicit other examples of rational or irrational thinking that would enhance or inhibit one's decision-making abilities. List sample sentences on the chalkboard.

3. Have students work with a partner to select any two or three positive self-talk sentences they feel would have a beneficial impact on their own decision-making process. Then ask each student to design and make a small poster displaying the pair's selected sentences.

4. Laminate student posters for display at home or school.

Discussion

Content Questions

1. How can rational thinking alter your feelings?
2. Can a change in how you're feeling affect your ability to make decisions? How?
3. Why is it sometimes important to know and practice some positive rational statements in advance of a decision-making moment?

Personalization Questions

1. Have you ever caught yourself using negative thinking in a decision-making moment? What effect did this have on your decision making?
2. Can you share a time when you used positive thinking to help you in your decision-making process?
3. What have you learned that you can apply in future situations?

To the Leader

Sample posters displaying positive rational thinking may be purchased from the Institute for Rational-Emotive Therapy, 45 East 65th Street, New York, NY 10021. Some would be suitable for general classroom display or for use as models for students' own posters.

One Step at a Time

Objective

To develop the ability to break problems into small, manageable parts

Materials

Main Problem Cards; tongue depressors, yarn, and markers as needed

Procedure

1. Present the students with a multistep math word problem (one in which they must perform at least three different operations to arrive at an answer). The following may serve as an example: Three people have been hired to paint a three-room office. Each office takes 2 gallons of paint, and each gallon costs 10 dollars. If each person gets paid 5 dollars an hour, and it takes 2 hours to do each room, what is the total cost of the job?

2. Analyze with students the process involved in arriving at a final solution. Stress that following and solving a sequence of subproblems was necessary before a final answer could be found.

3. Compare life decisions to the math problem by explaining that solving a life problem also often involves solving a sequence of smaller problems. Give the example of a student's selecting and purchasing a special gift for someone. Elicit and list the subproblems that might be involved, such as thinking about what the person likes, finding out whether the person already owns something similar, looking at the cost, determining how much you can afford, etc.

4. Divide students into pairs and give each pair a Main Problem Card. Encourage them to break this larger problem into subproblems.

5. After student pairs have discussed, analyzed, and listed the sequence of subproblems included in their main problem, have them make a Problem Ladder by gluing tongue depressors flat side out onto two parallel yarn strips, as illustrated. They can then print their sequence of subproblems, one per rung, onto the front side of the tongue depressors. The main problem should be printed on the uppermost rung.

6. Share completed Problem Ladders, then display.

Discussion

Content Questions

1. Was it difficult to break the main problem into smaller subproblems?
2. Why is it necessary to break problems down into smaller parts in order to solve them?
3. What can you do if a problem seems too big to solve all at once?
4. What would happen if you ignored or skipped over subproblems in an attempt to solve the main problem in a hurry?

Personalization Questions

1. Is there some personal problem you have that you seem unable to solve? Do you know all the subproblems involved, or have you missed some? Share examples.

To the Leader

The analytical thinking employed in this activity proves to be an essential life skill as well as an important study skill. It can be reinforced and practiced in the students' work in all content areas. In addition, it should also be stressed in the handling of personal and interpersonal problems arising in class.

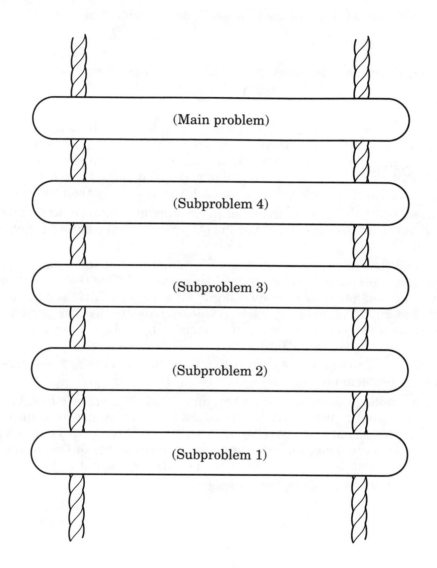

Main Problem Cards

Directions: Copy each problem on a separate index card.

Your little brother won't stay out of your room and your things.

You have to write a paper on a topic you know nothing about.

Your best friend wants to go along to a show, but you don't have an extra ticket.

You have to design an art project using "junk."

You want to learn to roller skate.

You lost directions to a friend's house, and you're supposed to go there after piano lessons.

You are home alone after school, and your cat is acting sick.

Your band lesson is today, and you forgot your drumsticks. You can't go home for them, and your parents are at work.

You like a certain girl/boy in your class and want her/him to start liking you.

You are in a small group working on the sports page for the class newspaper. Your assignment is due tomorrow, and you've hardly started.

You want to get elected class president.

Goal for It

Objective

To develop the ability to set short-term goals

Materials

Writing paper; wallpaper samples; stapler; colored markers

Procedure

1. Review the importance of breaking larger problems into subproblems to reach a final resolution, as introduced in Grades 5–6 Problem-Solving/Decision-Making Activity 5 (One Step at a Time).
2. Relate the analytical approach used in problem solving to goal setting. Stress the necessity of setting small, short-term subgoals to arrive at a larger, long-range goal.
3. Give an example of a long-range goal, such as getting straight *A*'s. Establish a sequence of short-term subgoals related to this larger goal. These subgoals might include listening in class, participating in discussions, making sure you understand directions, doing your homework and extra-credit work, studying for tests, and turning in assignments on time. List each subgoal on the chalkboard.
4. Supply students with several sheets of plain writing paper to fold and staple to make personal goal books. Use wallpaper samples for covers. Have each student print a title and his or her name on the front cover.
5. Have each student select a meaningful long-range goal and at least three short-term subgoals related to it. Instruct students to write these goals in their personal goal books. Students can then record their efforts and progress on their subgoals over a designated time period (2–3 weeks would be best).

Discussion

Content Questions

1. What was it like to record your efforts to reach subgoals? Did recording them help you keep more on track in terms of reaching your goal?
2. What is the best way to achieve a long-range goal? Why are such goals important?
3. What is the difference between a long-range goal and a short-term subgoal? Are the two related? How?

Personalization Questions

1. What long-range goals have you achieved in the past? How did you reach your goals? What subgoals did you set (consciously or unconsciously) to reach your main goal?
2. What subgoals are necessary for a long-range goal you have now? (Encourage students to think about such things as time, personal organization, and resources needed.)

To the Leader

It is important to review the goal books regularly to assess student comprehension and progress. To ease the time required to read each book and make appropriate individual comments, you can have 3–5 students turn in their books on a different assigned day. However it is managed, follow-up is essential.

INTERPERSONAL
RELATIONSHIPS

Choices, Choices Everywhere

Objective

To explore the pros and cons of various lifestyles

Materials

An assortment of current magazines; paper and markers; tagboard; brass brads; compasses; rulers; scissors; construction paper

Procedure

1. Distribute the magazines and have students cut out one picture of a person the student thinks looks interesting and appealing.

2. Distribute paper and direct the students through a character sketch of the person they selected. On the paper, they are to respond to the following questions.

   Where does this person live?

   What kind of work does this person do?

   What relationships does this person have with others? How does this person dress?

   What are this person's health habits like?

   What does this person do for recreation?

3. Allow students to share about their character.

4. Explain that what each student has imagined about his or her character constitutes a lifestyle. Stress that all persons have a certain, unique lifestyle they decide upon.

5. On the chalkboard, draw a large circle. Mark off pie sections and label each one with an aspect of lifestyle, as illustrated.

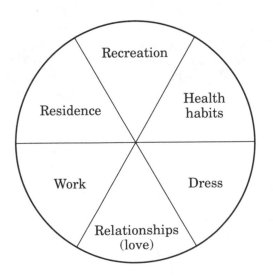

6. Discuss each category and brainstorm choices a person could make. For example, with regard to dress, a person could choose to wear jeans, dresses, slacks, long skirts, miniskirts, fur coats, jean jackets, etc.

7. Give each student a large piece of tagboard to make a personal Lifestyle Wheel. Instruct students to draw a circle with a compass, cut out the circle and section it into pie-shaped pieces with a ruler, and label each section with short phrases describing their choices for each of the categories established earlier. Have them attach a construction paper arrow with a brass brad at the center of their wheels.

8. Allow students to share their Lifestyle Wheels in small groups (4–6 participants) in game fashion. Each student is to spin the arrow on his or her wheel, then read aloud information recorded in whatever category the arrow points to. Other students must name the category being read from (recreation, relationships, etc.).

Discussion

Content Questions

1. On the Lifestyle Wheels, how many components make up a lifestyle?
2. Can you think of any lifestyle components that could be added?
3. Are there advantages to any of the choices you listed in each category? Are there any disadvantages? (For example, living in a city may be good because there are lots of fun things to do but bad because of the traffic and noise.)
4. When you make choices, should you consider only the advantages? Only the disadvantages? Both? Why?
5. Will any lifestyle choice be all positive? All negative?

Personalization Questions

1. How do you feel about your present lifestyle? How does your lifestyle compare to your family's lifestyle?
2. Has anyone ever criticized an aspect of your lifestyle? If so, how did you feel?
3. What did you learn from this activity?

To the Leader

In this activity, discussion may diverge in several ways. Students may focus on advantages and disadvantages of different lifestyles, or they may focus more on the variations in and assessment of lifestyle choices. Provided the direction is worthwhile, it may be advantageous to follow the students' lead and return to the lesson plan during a subsequent session.

Guessing Game

Objective

To learn that we aren't necessarily what others think we are

Materials

A cardboard box; selection of 5–6 common objects; paper and pencils as needed

Procedure

1. Place several common objects inside a cardboard box so students cannot see them. Items to be used might be a sponge, cotton swab, pencil, bar of soap, cracker, and roll of tape. Describe each item and have students attempt to guess what you're describing.

2. Direct a discussion relating the difficulty of naming the unseen items accurately to the process of forming an opinion of another person based only on what they say or do when we cannot really see or know what's inside them.

3. Have students compose sentences they might use to tell someone else about who they are. Instruct students to begin each listing with "I am" and encourage them to complete the sentence in as many different ways as possible. For example:

> I am a fifth grader.
>
> I am a good student.
>
> I am happy when I'm with my best friend.
>
> I am grouchy in the morning.
>
> I am a good basketball player.

Discussion

Content Questions

1. Why was it difficult to name the things inside the box?

2. If someone named the object incorrectly, did that prove the person was stupid? Did that necessarily mean the description was a bad one? Did the person's incorrect identification of the object change what the object really was in any way?

3. If someone is incorrect in their perception of who you are as a person, does that change who you really are?

4. Are we what people think we are?

5. Are people stupid or bad if they make wrong assumptions about who we are?

6. Are there ways we can change a wrong assumption? Can we always succeed in doing so?

7. What can we say to ourselves to feel OK, even if we have to live with someone's wrong ideas about us and cannot change those ideas?

Personalization Questions

1. Has anyone ever been wrong in their opinion about who you were?

2. How do you feel when someone makes wrong assumptions about you? What can you do about this?

To the Leader

Children at this age are becoming very susceptible to peer pressure. Encourage students to formulate sentences they can use to help feel good about themselves in the face of judgment or disapproval from others. As a follow-up activity, students could print their "emergency mental health sentences" on small posters or wallet-size cards.

One Plus One Plus One

Objective

To recognize that people can and will behave in different ways

Materials

Adding machine or other roll paper; pens or pencils as needed

Procedure

1. Select students to act out the following two scenarios.

    Scenario 1: A child brings home a stray dog and asks to keep it until the owner can be found. The parent expresses concern over who will care for the dog, offers to help share the responsibility, suggests they give the dog a bath together, and gets the dog some water.

    Scenario 2: A child brings home a stray dog and asks to keep it until the owner can be found. The parent gets upset, refuses to even consider it, and insists the child take the dog back to where he or she found it immediately and let it go.

2. On the chalkboard, write the following formula.

    Behavior = (Thoughts/Feelings) + (Past Experiences) + (Assumptions/Expectations)

    Use this formula as a means of directing an analysis of the scenarios to illustrate variations in human behavior. Sample behavior equations that may develop from analysis of each scenario would be as follows.

    Scenario 1: Parent says yes and offers to help = (I like dogs) + (I had a good dog when I was a kid) + (We can find the owner and help this dog)

    Scenario 2: Parent gets upset = (I dislike dogs) + (I got bit by a dog like this) + (This dog will cause trouble)

3. Distribute strips of roll paper. Instruct students to work in pairs to write two different behavior equations for two different possible reactions to the following open-ended scenario: "You come home from school with a note from the teacher saying you are failing science. Your parent . . ." Have students write the equations front to back on the length of paper provided.

4. Share completed equations and evaluate for inclusion of each element of behavior displayed in the model equation.

Discussion

Content Questions

1. What causes people to behave differently even in very similar situations?

2. Is it reasonable to expect people to behave exactly the same as other people? Why not?

3. Is it bad or wrong for a person to behave differently from what we may expect?

1. Has anyone ever surprised you by behaving or reacting in a way you did not expect? Why might they have acted as they did?

2. What can you do when someone behaves in a way you do not expect?

To the Leader

The elements of behavior presented in the model equation have been simplified for the purpose of this introductory lesson. The model suggests the elements are additive when, actually, they are causal in nature. (Past experiences may influence certain thoughts, which in turn influence feelings, etc.) This point is not important to make with students at this level, but the leader should keep it in mind.

Say What?

Objective

To learn effective interpersonal communication skills

Materials

Cue Cards; Scene Setter Cards; four large index cards per pair of students; pens or pencils as needed

Procedure

1. Select four volunteers and distribute a Scene Setter Card to one student and a Cue Card to each of the other three volunteers.

2. Each student with a Scene Setter Card studies his or her card and role plays the situation on it for each of the other three volunteers. These volunteers respond as instructed by their Cue Cards.

3. Discuss each role play as it is presented, identifying the interactive behaviors and listing them in one of the following four categories.

Positive verbal	Negative verbal
Examples: "I agree." "Can you explain?"	Examples: "Shut up." "That's stupid."
Positive nonverbal	**Negative nonverbal**
Examples: Smiles Nods yes	Examples: Crosses arms across chest Walks away, slams door

4. Repeat the process with new volunteers role playing and responding to the remaining two Scene Setter Cards.

5. Brainstorm and list other possible behaviors in each of the positive categories (verbal and nonverbal).

6. Supply each pair of students with four blank index cards and have them make up a Scene Setter Card and Cue Cards that stipulate only positive responses.

7. After completion, students exchange Scene Setter and Cue Cards and act out one anothers' specified interactions.

8. Follow each role play with a brief discussion, identifying the positive interactive behaviors demonstrated.

Discussion

Content Questions

1. Do you have a choice in how you react to and interact with others?
2. How does your choice of behaviors affect other people?
3. How can you become more positive in your verbal and nonverbal cues?
4. What are the advantages of becoming a more positive interactor?

Personalization Questions

1. Have you ever reacted positively to someone? How did that person behave in response?
2. Have you ever reacted negatively to someone? How did that person respond?
3. Which type of interaction do you prefer?

To the Leader

During discussion of the Personalization Questions, encourage students to share as many personal experiences as possible. Providing as many actual, real-life examples as possible will encourage application and transference to students' daily behavior.

Scene Setter Cards

Directions: Copy each each of the following situations on a separate index card.

Your dad asks you to help with the dishes when it's not your turn.

Your brother insists that you took his favorite album.

The teacher says your report needs revision.

Cue Cards

Directions: Copy each of the following responses on a separate index card.

Positive Cues

Ask questions to learn more about what the person is requesting.

Tell the person politely that you think there has been a mistake.

Go along with it.

Say what you think without getting upset.

Negative Cues

Leave the scene—walk away.

Argue, saying things like "No way. You're crazy!"

Get angry.

Refuse to talk or listen.

Solve It

Objective

To learn positive conflict resolution techniques

Materials

Problem Cards

Procedure

1. Assemble students in a circle and facilitate a discussion of typical problems they encounter in interpersonal relationships. Make a list of these on the chalkboard.

2. Divide students into triads and provide them with a Problem Card. Have the group discuss a positive solution to the problem situation. (These could also be role played.)

3. After 10 minutes, invite students to read their problem situations and share their solutions. Following each presentation, direct an analysis of the technique used to resolve the problem. Name these techniques and list them on the board. Examples of techniques include Compromise, Talk It Out, Take Some Space, Trial and Error, Alternatives, etc.

Discussion

Content Questions

1. What kinds of things typically cause problems in relationships?
2. What are some ways to overcome problems with other people?

Personalization Questions

1. Are there some problems you seem to encounter repeatedly in your relationships?
2. Why might some problems arise more often for you than for others?
3. Is there anything you could work on to reduce the number of problems you have with other people?
4. When you have a problem in a relationship, what do you usually do? Are your actions effective? What could you do instead that might be more effective?

To the Leader

The following conflict resolution techniques should be presented during the development of this activity: compromise; verbalization; attacking the problem and not the other person; allowing time and space to allow communication to proceed with less volatile overtones; trying different solutions; being willing to attempt new behaviors to see how they work out; and, finally, diplomatically terminating relationships that repeatedly dissolve into confrontation.

Problem Cards

Directions: Copy each situation on a separate index card.

You and a friend get along fine except when a certain third person starts to show interest in your friend. Then your friend starts to ignore you.

You and your mom can never agree on what kinds of clothes are OK for you to buy for school. You really dislike the things she picks out and feel embarrassed to wear them.

You shared something in confidence with your friend, then your friend told it to someone else. You try to talk about the situation but end up fighting.

You want to go skating this weekend, but your friend refuses, even though you did what he or she wanted to do last weekend.

Your friend becomes jealous because you seem to be the more popular of the two of you. Every time you try to talk about something exciting happening to you, your friend gets mad.

Your teacher always blames you for any trouble that happens in the class, even when it's not your fault.

You get along pretty well with everyone except one classmate, who usually makes fun of you in every class by making comments about your work.

Your dad wants you to go on a weekend vacation with the family, but you want to go to a friend's birthday party.

Tune It

Objective

To identify the characteristics of sensitivity to others

Materials

Paper and pencils as needed

Procedure

1. Have volunteers pantomime asking the class to do each of the following things.

   > Stand up and wave.

   > Applaud after walking an imaginary tightrope.

   > Repeat simple movements in follow-the-leader style.

   > Smile when they raise their right hands, nod when they raise their left hands.

2. Direct an analysis of how the person doing the pantomime communicated the message and discuss what was required of the class in order to understand.

3. Relate the pantomime activity to communication and response in relationships, using the Content Questions.

4. Have students write a paragraph describing someone they think is especially sensitive and responsive. They are to include examples of things that person does and how the person makes others feel. Share when complete.

Discussion

Content Questions

1. How did the people doing the pantomimes convey what they wanted?
2. In what other ways do people tell us what they want in real life?
3. What must you do in order to understand and be able to respond?

Personalization Questions

1. Have you ever known someone who was very good at figuring out what you needed or wanted, even if you didn't say how you felt in words? How do you suppose the person was able to do that?
2. How can someone best show understanding and caring about what you need or want?
3. How does it make you feel when others are sensitive to you and respond to your needs?
4. How do you feel when you are able to be sensitive to others you care about?
5. How can you be more sensitive to others?

To the Leader

The elements of attending, thinking, caring, and making a response comprise sensitivity to others. These should be drawn out and highlighted during the discussion. Encourage students to keep these elements in mind as they write their paragraphs.

INDEX OF ACTIVITIES

Accept or Change   183
Approach or Avoid   221
Assess the Decision   223

Beliefs, Feelings, and Behaviors   121
Big and Little Choices   57

Can Do, Can't Do   15
Cause and Effect   49
Changes, Changes   17
Changing Thoughts, Changing Feelings   193
Checking It Out   123
Choices, Choices Everywhere   237
Choosing to Behave   41
Consequences   215

Decisions and Consequences   53

Erase the Irrational   217
Exaggerations   47
Express It!   33

Face the Facts   153
Face Your Feelings   101
Fact or Fantasy   39
Facts and Beliefs   117
Feel Wheel   25
Feelings and Physical Reactions   199
For Better or Worse   137

Glad to Be Me   155
Goal for It   233
Guessing Game   239

Hand Me Some Happiness   75
Healthy/Unhealthy Expression   191
Help or Hinder?   189
How Do You Feel?   113
How Might They Feel?   197
How Strong?   105

I Am, I Do   173
I Can Try   95
I Feel, I Do   111
I Have to Have My Way   45
I Think, I Feel   103
If I Say So   227
I'm Afraid   35
It's Always   207
It's Awful!   129
It's Me!   157
It's OK to Goof Up   77

Judgment Machine   151
Just Different   87

Like 'Em or Not   31

Me Power   175
Mistakes Mean . . .   21
Multiple Solutions   59

Nobody Likes Me   89

One of a Kind   161
One Plus One Plus One   241
One Step at a Time   229
Once Upon a Time   135
Oops!   19
Options   127

People Hunt   11
People Poster   13
People Sorting   69
Perfectly, Perfectly   97
Performance Wheel   179
Plus or Minus Tac-Toe   79
Put-Downs   91

R and R   147
Rational or Irrational   203
React and Respond   145
Ripple Effect, The   141
Rose-Colored Glasses   211

Say What?   243
Sensible or Not Sensible?   43
Shoulds, Shoulds, Shoulds   209
So They Say   93
Solve It   245
Stop, Go, and Caution   125

Talking It Out   65
Thermometer of Emotions   107
They Made Me Feel   187
True Blue   165
Tune It   247

Voicebox   177

We Can If We Try   55
We All Have Feelings   27
What Happens When . . .   133
What Now?   61
What's Inside?   71
Where Do You Hurt?   29
Who Isn't What?   171
Why Judge?   73

Yours vs. Mine vs. Ours   225

ABOUT THE AUTHOR

Ann Vernon, Ph.D., is an associate professor and coordinator of counseling in the Department of Educational Administration and Counseling at the University of Northern Iowa, Cedar Falls. Dr. Vernon is the director of the Midwest Center for Rational-Emotive Therapy, an affiliate of the Institute for Rational-Emotive Therapy, founded by Dr. Albert Ellis. In addition, she is a therapist in private practice, working primarily with children and their families, and consults with teachers, parents, and mental health professionals on a variety of issues.

Dr. Vernon holds a doctorate in counseling and human development from the University of Iowa and has received advanced training in psychotherapy from the Institute for Rational-Emotive Therapy. She is the author of several emotional education programs for students, including *Help Yourself to a Healthier You* (Minneapolis: Burgess, 1989). Her current research interests focus on rational-emotive education with children, child stress, and consultation.